DODGEVILLE

CAPTURING HEARTS

By

Rick Birk

ISBN no. 978-0-9819964-6-2

Library of Congress Categories: Sports. Sports Nonfiction.
Sports events. Coaching. Ball games.

This book is easily available at go5books.com

Author's Note

As a youth, I had the opportunity to witness and experience an extraordinary period in Wisconsin high school basketball. Champions come and champions go. Most are revered for a time, but that reverence finds its way to the subsequent victors. There is one champion, however, that is different. The reverence remains to this day. As a die-hard player, coach, and fan of basketball, I have a distinct duty—no less than a moral obligation—to convey their storyline and reveal their precious gift.

I thank the Dodgeville teams of 1962-63 and of 1963-64 for giving me the honor of narrating their story and giving documentation to their legacy. This book is based entirely on true and factual information. I would like to thank everyone who took so much of their valuable time to contribute to this historical narrative.

Testimonials

"Rick Birk's portrayal of a small American town capturing a gold trophy against immense odds in high school basketball signifies one of the greatest achievements in the state of Wisconsin championship annals. I have had the sincere honor of meeting many of the members of the team and coaching staff over the years and they have all represented the city of Dodgeville in a first-class manner. Dennis Morgan, who played for Coach Wilson and graduated the year before the state championship, served as one of my assistant coaches at UW-Platteville. He told me many, many stories and showed me how much he learned from the Dodgeville coaching staff and his teammates. Long live the memories of this small community's success, when the world of Wisconsin high school basketball was all one class."

-Bo Ryan. A member of five basketball Halls of Fame and the winner of numerous Coach of the Year honors, Coach Ryan has entered his 13th season guiding the Wisconsin program in November, 2013. Ryan began his college coaching career at UW-Platteville in 1984. In fifteen years as Pioneers coach, he compiled a remarkable 314-37 record, winning eight WIAC titles and four national championships. In 1999 Ryan moved on to UW-Milwaukee for a two-year period, leading the Panthers to two winning seasons. In 2001, he became the University of Wisconsin head coach. Here he found immediate success, as his 2001-02 team shared the Big Ten championship, the first at Wisconsin in fifty-five years. In his second season his team won a school record 24 games and an outright Big Ten title. In both these seasons the Badgers were invited to the NCAA Tournament and Ryan was named Big Ten Coach of the Year. Since arriving in Madison, Ryan has won five Big Ten titles and has taken his teams to the NCAA tournament twelve straight years. His career record stands at 674-216. His career winning percentage of .757 ranks in the top ten among all-time coaches with over 600 career wins. Coach Ryan was named Big Ten Coach of the Year again in the 2012-13 campaign.

"From one small school to another—congratulations on your accomplishment. Big things do come in small packages. Follow your dreams."

-Bobby Plump - Famed 1954 Milan, IN, high school star whose last-second winning shot was portrayed by Jimmy Chitwood in the movie 'Hoosiers.'

Testimonials

"This book and the many main characters will touch many emotionally, just as many were touched over fifty years ago. Judging from the comments and the lives of so many of those who were there, the message lives on! John "Weenie" Wilson resonated with me then, and remains with me now."

-Dick Bennett - Dick Bennett won 489 games in his college coaching career. At NAIA Steven's Point his 1983-84 team was national runner-up and Bennett was named NAIA Coach of the Year. Moving on to UW-Green Bay in 1985, he next built the Phoenix into a mid-major power and led his 1990-91 Green Bay team to its first NCAA tournament berth. In 1993-94, his 12th-seeded Phoenix defeated 5th-seeded California with Jason Kidd in the opening round of the NCAA tournament. In 1995 Coach Bennett moved on to the University of Wisconsin-Madison. Replacing Stan Van Gundy, he led his team to an NIT berth in his first year and then on to three NCAA tournament appearances, including a final-four appearance in the 1999-2000 season. After taking two years off, he finished his coaching career as the head coach at Washington State University. In 2006, the program was taken over by his son, Tony. The winner of numerous "Coach of the Year" awards, Bennett was the recipient of the "National Coach Wooden Keys to Life Award" at the 2013 Final Four.

"*Dodgeville: Capturing Hearts* puts power behind the words 'hard work pays off.' A real life David versus Goliath encounter, the book not only captivates its readers, but inspires them to do great things. The Dodger's year long journey from a small-town second place team to state champions is truly astounding. This novel is a must read for any sports fan."

-Mike Fink - Mike Fink is in his 14th year as Athletic Director at Kettle Moraine High School in Wales, WI. In his twenty-five years at Kettle Moraine, Mike has coached basketball, baseball and was the head football coach for 13 years. Twenty-four years ago, Mike established the school's first girls' fast-pitch program and was head coach for 17 seasons. Mike also created and implemented the Kettle Moraine off campus Alternative School fourteen years ago. Over100 students have graduated from that facility.

Testimonials

"Wisconsin is a beautiful state! It has four seasons—winter, spring, summer and fall. All have their own beauty, but winter has its own distinctives—high school basketball and ice fishing!! On those winter nights from November through March, high school basketball is king. The writer of this story has captured the hearts of one Wisconsin small town which lived a State Championship and a 26-0 perfect season! It is a great story. Having coached two Wisconsin high schools (Stevens Point and Beloit) to the state tournament in Madison in earlier years, I can feel the Dodgeville story. As the TV analyst for several years at the tournament, I had the privilege to become acquainted with players, coaches and fans from all over the entire state. Coach Wilson and the Dodgeville story were unique and inspiring. You do not want to miss this story."

-John Erickson - A Little All-American at Beloit College, Erickson coached high school basketball at both Beloit and Stevens Point, taking both schools to state. After serving two years in the army, he coached at Lake Forest College for three years before moving on to the University of Wisconsin as an assistant. The following year he succeeded Bud Foster as the Badger head coach for nine seasons. His 1961-62 team finished second in the conference. In 1968, Erickson became the General Manager of the Milwaukee Bucks expansion team. In 1970, he resigned to run for the U.S. Senate. Subsequently, he lost his bid to incumbent William Proxmire. Erickson later became the president of The Fellowship of Christian Athletes, a position he would hold for a fifteen-year period.

"Having been a part of Wisconsin small-town basketball for forty-six years, I believe that Birk captures the pride and essence of small-town Wisconsin with this inspiring story. As an eyewitness to the championship game back in 1964, I can attest to Dodgeville's improbable victory as truly one for the ages. This book is a great read that all Wisconsin basketball fans will fall in love with."

-Jerry Petitgoue - A 46-year veteran of Wisconsin high school basketball, the legendary Petitgoue is starting his 43rd year at Cuba City. He is the winningest high school coach in Wisconsin basketball history, with 846 victories. His Cuba City teams have won three state titles. Petitgoue, 73, is currently the Executive Director of the Wisconsin Basketball Coaches Association.

Testimonials

"It was a special time to grow up in Dodgeville in the 1960s. I was three years old when Dodgeville won the State Basketball Championship. Rick's book connects the dots on how this fabulous story could take place. Coach Wilson played professional football and baseball. That speaks to his knowledge of sports and competitive nature. The 1964 team was loaded with three-sport star athletes. My friends and I played football, basketball or baseball every day of the year. Dodgeville was that kind of town. I always wanted to be a coach. The readers will enjoy this fascinating book, a small-town Norman Rockwell. The Dodgeville schools should put it in their history curriculum."

-Neal Nelson - A 1973 graduate of Dodgeville High School, Neal Nelson was an all-conference shooting guard and captain of Coach Bob Buck's Conference championship team. Neal is the winningest men's basketball coach in Wisconsin junior college history with 534 wins in thirty years at the University of Wisconsin-Waukesha. Coach Nelson was inducted into the Wisconsin Basketball Coaches Association Hall of Fame in 2012.

"*Dodgeville: Capturing Hearts* is a wonderful story of a small town in Wisconsin and a very special coach, John "Weenie" Wilson. Wilson's Dodger team was the state runner-up in 1963 and won the state championship in 1964. Remarkably, this was accomplished in a single-class tournament. Birk has done an excellent job describing Coach Wilson, the players, and all of the Dodgeville people involved in this wonderful story. In 1963 my Fennimore High School team played against Wilson's Dodgers, losing to them in overtime. The following year we again lost to them in the tournament. As a coach who knew Wilson quite well, I can honestly say Rick Birk captured the heart and soul of Dodgeville Coach John "Weenie" Wilson. His book is a must read."

-Eli Crogan - Eli Crogan is a 1996 member of the Wisconsin Basketball Coaches Hall of Fame. Winning 562 prep games, he spent twenty-two years at Watertown High School, in addition to stops at Soldiers Grove, Fennimore and Wayland Academy. He also led the University of Wisconsin-Whitewater program from 1970-1974, compiling a 68-29 record where his teams were co-conference champions in his last two seasons. From 1975-1977, Crogan scouted for the NBA Houston Rockets. He is currently the Wisconsin State Mentoring Director and is Chairman of the WBCA Mr. Basketball Committee.

Acknowledgments

George Faherty
Farness Studios
Mike Fink
Juanita First
Michael FitzGibbons
Donna (Schill) Glanville
Tony Goedheer
Mike Grainger
Green Bay Packers
Eric Hagerup
Christine (Humbert) Harrison
Jayne Harrison
Janette Hartman
Betty Heim
Ray Heim
Bill Helin
Ginnie (Arthur) Helin
Anna Hendrickson
Roger Hirstein
Barry Hottmann
Missy Hottmann
Vicki (Atkinson) Hugill
Mark Hutchinson
Iowa County Historical Society
Randy Jackson
John Johnson
Sheri Johnson
John Jung

Robert Jung
Jim Keyes
Vicki (Evans) Keyes
Larry Klarner
Mary (Keyes) Leonard
Brian Lucas
Lavern Luebstorf
Betty (Baumgardt) Luedtke
Dr. Rolf Lulloff
Lee Lurvey
Manitowoc High School
Barry Marks
Robert Masters
Dennis McCormick
Bob McGraw
Diane McGraw
Kathryn McGraw
Margaret McGraw
Bob McNeill
Jim Meyers
Charlie Miller
Dianne (Peterson) Mingione
Tony Mooren
JoMarie Morgan
Ned Moton
Mort Moyer
Ronald Murphy
Merlin Nadler

Acknowledgments

Vicky (Meuer) Nadler

Tom Neises

Neal Nelson

Neville Public Museum

Todd Novak

Pat Obma

Vern Ott

Jeanne (Schmoekel) Paquin

Jack (John) Paulin

Jerry Petitgoue

Louise Pfotenhauer

Donald Pick

Bobby Plump

Andy Ptak

Otto Puls

Mike Reilly

Royce Reukauf

Richland Center High School

Kelly Ritchie

Bob Rundle

Dick Rundle

Denny Rundle

Bo Ryan

Carrie Schroeder

Deb Schwarz

Julie Seidel

Blanton Simmons

Bill Singer

Tim Singer

Vickie (Reynolds) Stangel

Tom Stephens

Dave Stocks

Chuck Tank

Nancy Tiegs

Tammy Townsend

University of Wisconsin

Jan (Kobbervig) Uselmann

Ross Vivian

Scott Von Rueden

Marcia Wagner

Scott Walker

Gari Walz

Julie Weiskircher

James Whitford

Earl Williams

Anne Wilson

Dennis Wilson

Richard Wilson

Pat Woods

www.southernvisions.net - Cover Photo

Special Acknowledgement

A special recognition is in order for all the members of the 1962-63 and 1963-64 Dodgeville basketball teams. A WIAA ruling allowed only twelve players to be active on a team roster for state tournament play in Madison. Generally, most squads were comprised of several more players during the regular season. It is essential that all the members be mentioned as each made his own individual contribution to the Dodgeville story. We also would like to acknowledge 1962-63 assistant coach John Crubaugh for his selfless dedication to the Dodgeville sports programs.

Bob Anderson	Ken Johanning
Curtis Anderson	Ron Maines
Rick Brown	Dennis Morgan
Craig Brue	Brian Olson
Tom Brunker	Bill Polkinghorn
Bob Campbell	Steve Rasmussen
Mike Collins	Pat Reilly
Ron Dickinson	Bob Rock
Corky Evans	Kramer Rock
Patrick Flynn	Tom Schleck
Mike Gust	Steve Schroeder
Bill Harris	Dick Stephens
Bruce Harrison	Danny Stombaugh
Duane Honerbaum	Larry Wagner
Tom Hughes	Scott Wichman
David Johanning	

Dedication

To Coach Wilson and all those who share a special love of basketball. As players, coaches, referees, fans and families, we realize that the beauty of the game lies within its fundamental skills, precise teamwork, and the motivation of its athletes. When each of these components works in concert with one another and are accomplished at a maximum level, the result can be a brilliant masterpiece, comparable to the work of a Picasso. We must all work collectively to preserve this treasure in time.

John "Weenie" Wilson

Prologue

In March, 1963, the Dodgeville Dodgers marched into Madison, Wisconsin as a member of the remaining field of eight at the Wisconsin high school boys' basketball championships. With a school population of just 395 students, they were paired against opponents from much-larger populated schools, some exceeding 1800 students. Regardless, this group of mighty mites used this disparity as motivation in their quest for a state championship. Led by their future Hall of Fame coach John "Weenie" Wilson, they fought their way to the title game. Despite a gallant effort, their dream would end in a defeat by Manitowoc, by a score of 74-52. It would now take another year before they would again earn an opportunity to contend for the title and, this time, a chance for redemption. *Could* they finally achieve the impossible dream?

This is their story.

Chapter One

To this day, I consider myself very fortunate. My whole life I have been surrounded by outstanding citizens and role models; some I have known personally and others I have admired from afar. However, I can't say it has always been easy to pick them out amid the turmoil, sensationalism, and negative news that permeate our society on a daily basis. None-the-less, if one has an open mind and the wherewithal to seek out the genuineness of these people and what they truly stand for, he will most definitely find that they do exist and their message will resonate. When they do finally appear to us and we ascertain a conscious knowing of their precious gifts, we subsequently have the capability to grasp these special bequests and append them to our own character. Moreover, when someone shares something of value with you and you benefit from it, you have a moral obligation to share it with others. Herein lies my motivation for telling this story.

In March of 1963, I was between sports seasons. As an eleven-year-old sixth-grader at Cushing Elementary School in Delafield, Wisconsin, we had finished our basketball season a few weeks earlier. Our season had been a huge success. Most of my teammates including Lee, Dave, and Tony as well as myself seemed to be gaining a true understanding of the game and its true fundamentals thanks to our coach, Donald Pick, a seventh-grade teacher at our school. Our three-man weave had grown to a five-man weave, our left hands had matured from that awkward stage, and our free throw shooting had become second to none.

I was getting antsy. It would now be at least three weeks before I could run outside to throw a baseball. My prized Milwaukee Braves' baseball cap and jacket would remain on the hook, on hold a little longer. For now, I would settle for shoveling the snow from our driveway each afternoon after school and practicing my set shot for hours on our garage hoop.

Thanks to my older brother Tom, a sophomore varsity basketball player at St. John's Military Academy in Delafield, I had been privileged to get sports instruction at an early age. With his knowledge and the talk from my classmates at school, I learned that this day, Thursday, March 14, would be the first day of the final leg of the boys' state basketball championship in Madison, Wisconsin. How lucky we were that most of the games would be televised on WITI-TV, Channel 6. Each year all the public schools, regardless of school size or record, were given the opportunity to start fresh at the end of the regular season and compete in the one giant winner-take-all state basketball tournament. This protocol had come from a Wisconsin Interscholastic Athletic Association philosophy that gave hope to teams that may have struggled early in the season but had made significant progress during the course of the year. Brackets and pairings for all the schools had been published in the *Milwaukee Journal* three weeks earlier, days before the first games were to be played. Over a three-week period, some 400 public school teams throughout the state had met in fierce battles, with the winners moving on to live another day. The action had moved from the local sub-regional tournaments to the regional finals, then to the sub-sectionals and sectional finals, where today's eight sectional winners would be vying for the state championship. These final eight teams, along with their schoolmates, families, and fans, would make the trip to the University of Wisconsin Field House for an unforgettable episode of excitement and pageantry that only high school basketball can provide. This old structure, nicknamed UW Fieldhouse, had broken ground in 1929 and opened its doors in 1930. Its construction cost was a mere $434,000 and it offered a seating capacity of 11,500. The WIAA Boys State Basketball Tournament had found its home here in the years 1930-35 and 1937-1997. (The structure has since given way to the new state-of-the-art Kohl Center, which opened its doors in 1998.)

But back to 1963: Today's competition would feature highly ranked Milwaukee North and Racine Horlick; Manitowoc would battle Superior Central; Dodgeville would take on Clintonville; and lastly, Eau Claire would meet Beloit. Even though I was watching the games on our 14-inch black-and-white Zenith, I could feel the excitement in the air amid the sounds of the loud Field House horn and the cheers of the crowd, products of each thrilling moment.

In the first afternoon game of the day, once-defeated Milwaukee North was upset by unranked Racine Horlick 51-50. A 25-foot jump shot by Gary Pinnow with only three seconds left stunned the only undefeated team making its way to Madison. The game had been tied at 44-44 at the end of regulation, requiring an overtime period. Here the score changed hands a few times before Pinnow drilled his jumper from just left of the free throw circle.

In the afternoon's second game, Manitowoc outlasted Superior Central. To counter a 9-point lead by Superior Central at the break, Manitowoc surged with about four minutes to go in the contest, cutting the lead to 55-50. Key plays by John Lallensack in the final minutes gave Manitowoc a 61-58 lead with 31 seconds remaining. The Ships then padded their lead with a series of free throws as Superior was forced to foul. The final score was 64-58.

After a break came the night games, the first featuring the Clintonville Truckers and the Dodgeville Dodgers. As the game began, both teams prodded offensively, looking for openings. A Trucker lead of 13-8 in the first quarter changed dramatically as Dodger Rick Brown scored three points to cut the lead to two. Now teammate Pat Flynn started to come on strong. With a minute left in the quarter, he hit three straight jumpers, allowing the Dodgers to secure a 19-12 lead as the quarter expired. The momentum for Dodgeville continued into the second quarter as Flynn stayed hot, scoring 14 points in the first half giving the Dodgers a 37-27 lead at the break. Clintonville was determined to get back in the game and fought back valiantly in the third period. However, towards the end of the third quarter, Dodger 5'9" point guard Bruce Harrison took over, scoring 13 points to rally the Dodgers and put the game out of reach for the Truckers. The final score was Dodgeville 69 and Clintonville

52. Harrison and Bill Polkinghorn made an incredible 18 of 20 free throws for the night. Dodgeville shot 40.4 percent from the floor while out-rebounding the Truckers by a 52-28 margin. Clintonville made only one less field goal for the game, but lagged dramatically in free throws by a 27-12 margin. Flynn led Dodgeville with 16 points, while Harrison chipped in 13. Melzer was high for Clintonville with 18.

Although Dodgeville had appeared to start slowly during the contest, their coach Wilson, when interviewed, insisted that it had nothing to do with jitters. "We have been doing that all year," he replied. "I don't know why, but our boys are men now. They weren't scared." The coach went on to mention how his team practices during their lunch hour back at school. "All the players bring their lunch to school and then we get 15 to 20 minutes of practice then. We only have an hour or so after school before our boys, most of whom are farm lads, have to catch the bus home."

The final game of the night featured Eau Claire and Beloit. The Old Abes from Eau Claire turned a close game into a convincing win by hitting 10 of 16 shots in the final period, bringing their field goal percentage to a noteworthy 52 percent for the game. The game had been tied at the end of the third quarter before Eau Claire made its surge and won by a 73-66 margin. Vern Curtis scored a game high of 25 points while Ron Mitchell chipped in 19. Gerry Kenney led Beloit with 21.

As the games ended for the night, it didn't take me long to choose the team I would now root for. Even though I had watched every game intently, I seemed to be mesmerized by one team in particular, the Dodgeville Dodgers. Why? I can't say for sure. Maybe it was the way they approached the game. They came from a small town as I did and they were definite underdogs. Yet they seemed extremely poised and confident. They arrived in Madison with a 21-1 record, their only loss coming in overtime from an inspired Darlington team. Winners of the Southwest Wisconsin Athletic League (SWAL), the Dodgers were on the march led by their coach, John (Weenie) Wilson, a seasoned veteran. However, their path to Madison had not been an easy one. They had won a slow-down triple-overtime barnburner with Lancaster (37-33), a team they had earlier faced and defeated during the regular season. Lancaster's Coach Paulin, much like Wilson, was always prepared, and his team went toe-to-toe with the Dodgers until the very end. The Dodgers then blew out Darlington the following game by a score of 65-30 in the sub-regional, a team that had given them their only loss of the year. This had been their third meeting of the year with Darlington, coached by Richard (Dick) Davies, who had played at Dodgeville and is a member of the Dodgeville Hall of Fame. They subsequently prevailed in overtime to defeat Fennimore, another league foe, in the regional final 40-35, making their way to the sub-sectional. After trailing in the first game of the sub-sectional for three quarters, they defeated a stubborn Belmont team by 62-53. They next defeated Coach Wilson's hometown of Richland Center 71-65 before upsetting favorite Monroe in the sectional final 64-

50. As 1963 Dodgeville player Pat Reilly recalls the Monroe upset, "Our point guard, Denny Morgan, had a great night and led us in scoring. I also scored, Rick Brown owned the boards, and Pat Flynn and Duane Honerbaum contributed on offense and defense." Reilly recounted the locker room scene after the game. "Don Lindstrom from the *Wisconsin State Journal* came into the locker room to interview Coach Wilson. I heard him say 'You have a real star there.' He meant Morgan, but Weenie just looked at him and said, 'Which one?' I guess that was one of the greatest things about playing for Coach Wilson. He asked us *all* to perform and we did."

The scene was tense outside the gym after Dodgeville's victory over Monroe. One account holds that Monroe students were waiting for Dodger students as they attempted to board their bus and a fight ensued. With a huge crowd and so much on the line, tempers had been flaring all evening.

Leading the Dodgeville 1963-1964 team were captains Pat Reilly and Duane Honerbaum. Reilly was the team's leading scorer at 15 points per game, while Rick Brown was second at 14. The same two were also the team's leading rebounders with Brown pulling down 10 rebounds per game while Reilly was just behind him with 9. Co-captain Reilly related what Coach Wilson had informed the team prior to the Madison trip, "We are among the last eight teams to be playing and only one of those would end the season with a win." Yes, the Dodgers were now in elite company.

When the Dodgeville team finally arrived at the

tournament in Madison for its initial walk-through of the huge, empty Wisconsin Field House, the team was in for a big laugh. Junior team member Corky Evans, from a Dodgeville farming family, is said to have viewed the large arena with awe-filled trepidation and remarked, "Boy Coach, you sure could put a lot of hay in this place!" Senior Bill Polkinghorn added, "Coming from a small town and playing in a small gym, then stepping onto a college-size floor, was a little overwhelming. But like Coach Wilson said, 'The other team can only play five at a time, just like we do.'"

As Day Two began, the losers from Day One met in the afternoon consolation bracket while the four winners moved on in the winners' bracket and would be featured in the night games. North won the first game of the day, outlasting Superior Central by a score of 74-71. In the second consolation game, Beloit got by an equally stubborn Clintonville by a 69-64 margin.

As the night tournament games got underway, the first semi-final featured Manitowoc and Racine Horlick. The Manitowoc Ships' taut zone forced Horlick to shoot from the outside. In addition, they often surprised the Racine team with a suffocating press. However, it was not until the third quarter that Manitowoc took control. Thanks to the rebounding of Bob Duvall and John Lallensack, John Neilitz was able to score several fast-break baskets, allowing the Ships to outscore Horlick 23-16 in the third quarter and gradually pull away. The final score was Manitowoc 66 and Racine Horlick 52. Duvall led the Ships with 19 points while

Mike Mucklin matched his total and led Horlick with 19.

As the final game of the night was approaching, I could hardly wait for Dodgeville to take the floor. This small school had been getting a great deal of attention in the media and around the state. They were becoming the tournament darling.

Eau Claire and Dodgeville were very well matched, and the game was close the entire way. The Dodgers were very deliberate on offense in an effort to secure good looks. Defensively they zoned Eau Claire, making them shoot from the outside. Unfortunately for Eau Claire, Vern Curtis, who had scored 27 points in the opening round, was off the mark against the Dodgers missing 11 of 16 attempts. The lead changed hands eight times in the last quarter alone. With two minutes left to go, Pat Flynn intercepted a pass and Duane Honerbaum turned the possession into a huge basket with slightly over a minute to go. With fourteen seconds left, Bruce Harrison secured a rebound off a missed jumper by Eau Claire's Ron Mitchell. Harrison, who had won the team's annual free throw trophy, hit two clutch charity shots to give the Dodgers a 3-point lead at 52-49. A late tip-in just before the final horn by Eau Claire's Jim Long cut the final margin to a point. Dodgeville had prevailed by the slimmest of margins 52-51. Pat Flynn led Dodgeville with 17 points and 10 rebounds. Rick Brown chipped in 16 points and picked up 9 rebounds.

The semi-final game with Eau Claire took its toll on Dodgeville's Coach Wilson. Exhausted from his team's one-point victory over the Old Abes, he seriously considered not coaching his team in Saturday's state championship game against Manitowoc. "I'm awfully tired," said Wilson, "I may not be able to make it tomorrow night. I will need an awful lot of rest." Two years earlier Wilson had suffered not one but two heart attacks and had spent over two months in an oxygen tent in critical condition at Appleton Memorial Hospital. Despite his health concerns, Coach was back to school on the first day as usual, teaching and coaching. Coach Wilson was said to be proud of the fact that his brush with death never caused him to miss a day of employment.

The final day of play began on Saturday, March 16, 1963. Three games were left to be played. In the first game, North Division beat Beloit by a score of 72-59. Winning the consolation title, North improved its record for the year to a remarkable 25-1. Game two, for third place, was a close game all the way, with Eau Claire nipping Racine Horlick 75-72. Eau Claire shot over 50 percent from the floor. Eau Claire's Vern Curtis led all scorers with 28 points.

Finally it came—the last game of the night and tournament, the state championship game for all the marbles. "Biggest School Plays Smallest for the Title" was the caption of the *Milwaukee Journal* article on that day. Manitowoc had the largest enrollment of schools in the tournament with 1837 students while Dodgeville had the smallest, at 395. Dodgeville also had the opportunity to become the first team since the 1959 Lincoln team to win the title in a school's first appearance at state. Manitowoc, ranked seventh with a

21-3 record, would be a difficult opponent for the sixteenth-ranked Dodgers, 23-1. I remember hoping that Dodgeville would be up for to the task right from the start, but I knew Manitowoc was a formidable opponent.

Dodgeville's 1963-64 Assistant Coach John Crubaugh, who later went on to become the superintendent of schools in of all places, Manitowoc, told of a pregame conversation he had with Coach Wilson regarding Manitowoc. "During our meeting at the AG dorms on campus the night after we had beaten Eau Claire, I told Coach among other things that I didn't think there was much we could do to beat them. We didn't match up well and our zone wasn't going to slow them down and we sure as hell couldn't play man-to-man, because we were slow and hadn't played it all year. He asked me about holding the ball against them and I answered him that it would lower the final score, but it wouldn't be fun for our kids or all the spectators, and right now we were the tourney darlings and we wouldn't be, two minutes into our stall."

As Manitowoc and Dodgeville took the floor, the TV camera panned the Dodgeville bench and I soon noticed that Coach Wilson was in attendance. Wilson had been advised, but not ordered by his doctor, to stay home and avoid the excitement of the game. Wilson chose to disregard his advice and coach the game. It now was game on before an excited crowd of 13,217. Pat Reilly, a 1963 Dodger starter, informed me that before the game Coach Wilson's brother-in-law, who sat on the bench as a precaution, had asked Pat and teammate Bill Polkinghorn to help him get Coach off the floor right after the game.

Coach John Jung, the skipper of the Manitowoc Ships, was quite confident his team would come out firing on all cylinders. Quite the contrary, the Ships started cold working against the Dodgeville zone defense, making a paltry 8 out of 28 attempts in the first half. Dodgeville was also forced to shoot from the outside against the Manitowoc zone, likewise without great success. However, the Ships were able to beat the Dodgers down the court several times on their fast break and to steal the ball at least a half dozen times using their occasional press. These two factors allowed the Ships to carry a 25-22 lead into half-time in a game that seesawed back and forth. As Dodgeville's Bill Polkinghorn remembered, "Coach Wilson was disappointed that we gave up a fast-break layup at the buzzer, as it would have been a one point-game. Due to his medical condition Coach knew he could not be his aggressive self."

In the third quarter the Ships finally lived up to their coach's billing. They regained their strength around the basket as well as their shooting touch. A three-point play at the end of the quarter extended their lead to nine points. For the quarter they made 9 of their 18 attempts and seemed to be back in rhythm. With the Ships on a roll, it was now difficult for the Dodgers to control the tempo.

As the fourth quarter began, the Ships reeled off seven unanswered points building a sixteen-point lead and putting the game virtually out of reach for Dodgeville. The combination of Lehman, Buchholz and Lallensack playing at such a high level made it difficult for the Dodgers to concentrate solely on just one or two of the Ship players. The final score was 74-52. Lehman led Manitowoc in scoring with 15 while Buchholz had 13. Lallensack scored 10 points and pulled down 14 rebounds. Brown led Dodgeville with 13 points. For the night the Ships shot 45 percent from the field, while Dodgeville finished with a mark of 38 percent.

Manitowoc was a great team and deserved to win. They came out like gangbusters in the second half and finished the job. The 1963 state title and the Gold Ball trophy was theirs.

I remember feeling Dodgeville's pain and sensing their strength when they accepted the runner-up trophy with the grace and class of a true champion. They had experienced a tremendous year and were simply beaten by a great team. Besides, who really expected this tiny school to contend with powerful Manitowoc?

I asked player Corky Evans what it was like to play in the huge UW-Madison Field House. "It was awesome," he told me. "Soooo much space after playing in the smaller local gyms. The roar of the crowd could be deafening. From the floor, the stands appeared completely dark. I could not see anyone in the bleachers." Teammate Pat Reilly remarked, "We were disappointed after the loss, but the Field House was packed with people who were there to see if we could beat the bigger school—Manitowoc ... and they let us know they were behind us." Dodger player Bill Polkinghorn offered, "After the game, Coach had a handshake, a hug and a thank you for each and every player." Junior Pat Flynn added, "I think over all we were proud to have gotten to the championship game." I asked him what Wilson had said to the team. He replied, "I don't think he said a lot, as he knew we were just overmatched by Manitowoc."

However, not only was this lopsided loss overwhelming for the whole Dodgeville contingency, but for seniors Denny Morgan, Duane Honerbaum, Dave Johanning, Brian Olson, Pat Reilly, and Bill Polkinghorn, this signaled the end of their high school basketball careers. This must have weighed heavily on their minds as they endured the two-hour bus ride back to Dodgeville. But it wasn't all sadness. Reilly added this insight: "The disappointment was lessened on the ride home. At the time the highway ran through the towns of Ridgeway, Barneveld, Mount Horeb and Verona. In every town the streets were lined with people cheering for us. Coach Wilson said, 'This is what it is all about. Someday you will know what you accomplished.'" Bill Polkinghorn saw it this way: "A loss is a loss is a loss. Not until we returned home did I realize the feat accomplished. Bitter archrivals were there congratulating and celebrating with us."

Moreover, could it be that this 1962-63 team and all this shared experience of getting so close could set the stage for better tomorrows? No, these seniors never got to bask in the glory of a state championship, but were the true pioneers playing a solid and integral part of providing a rock foundation on which others could now build. (See the appendix for a complete listing of all team members.)

Upon arriving home the Ships were treated to a huge

celebration. The seven car caravan that left Madison was estimated by police to be five miles long by the time it reached the Manitowoc city limits. Sunday saw a city-wide celebration where Coach Jung was presented a massive aluminum key to the city.

Sadly, Manitowoc coach John Jung passed away in March of 2011. Recently I was able speak with his son Robert. As a boy of 13, Robert attended most games and practices—a true coach's son. He told me, "I was blessed to be the son of a great coach and a great man. Growing up watching high school basketball was a thrill, and the memories still send chills up and down my body."

I asked Robert to give me his dad's assessment of the final game and the fact that they were flat in the first half. He recounted, "Dad was very concerned. We were not playing well and needed a spark. Thankfully we put it together in the second half. My dad was an emotional man and was very happy after the game. Dad believed in basics—ball-handling, passing and defense. He did not believe in yelling at players but in teaching them the right way to play the game and act on the floor. He was a big believer in planning and preparation. He almost never got out-coached. Dad didn't know Coach Wilson before the tournament, but had a lot of respect for him after. He thought they were alike in a lot of ways."

Then Robert added a bit of trivia. "It is ironic that before the 1962-63 season began, my dad had told the family he had accepted the athletic director's job and would be stepping down as coach next year. In addition, our key player, John Lallensack, hadn't played basketball as a sophomore. Dad was alerted to his playing city-league ball. Lallensack played JV ball as a junior before making his way to varsity as a senior and becoming All-State. He then went on to become an NAIA All-American at UW-Oshkosh."

Yes, hearts were broken, dreams lost, and hopes diminished for Dodgeville, their families and fans. But for me it had been an unbelievable tournament, full of a degree of excitement that I had not anticipated and that I hoped would last forever. It was now time to say goodbye to the Dodgeville Dodgers and thank them for a job well done. Little did I know that I, along with thousands of other Wisconsinites, had begun to form a bond with this team and this very special time of the year.

Chapter Two

et in the heartland some fifty miles southwest of Madison, midway between the state capital and Dubuque, Iowa, Dodgeville in 1963 was a typical Midwestern town. Subject to temperature extremes of the Great American Prairie (101° in 1988, -32° in 1994), the town was equally a cross-section of some 2,900 unique personalities. Much as the earth of the area fertilizes a wide variety of crops, the folks of Dodgeville embraced the traditional all-American values of faith, hard work, and family. Like the earth itself, Dodgeville residents were in many ways close to the elements. Agriculture is to this day an honored profession. Every summer brings a "Farmers' Appreciation Day," with a parade down Iowa Street and a festival in Harris Park. As the county seat, the city provides vital services for farmers—and is also the international headquarters for the clothing firm Lands' End. A uniquely structured corporation, Lands' End is passionate about each item it sells. The company believes in world-class customer service and gives an unconditional guarantee of product satisfaction. These old-fashion values are a perfect match for the hard-working, compassionate people of Dodgeville. Today, Dodgeville numbers approximately 5,000 residents.

Dodgeville is an ideal place to raise a family. There is a sense of consistency and of character that seems unaltered by time. Beliefs and customs are handed down from generation to generation and family ancestry can go back for many decades. It's a place where one can expect to receive a "hello" from a total stranger. It is the combination of shared values and close community, of pitching in and helping, of weathering hard times together, that explains the town's success. One who looks deeper into the community may better understand the values that exist and uncover the cornerstones of success.

I had the opportunity to chat with 1964 Dodger alum Ginnie (Arthur) Helin and her husband Bill, a 1962 Dodgeville graduate. Bill currently owns and manages Helin Appraisal Services. Ginnie recalled the social climate during her time as a cheerleader in 1963 and 1964. "In Dodgeville people were kind to each other," she put it. "Family values were first and foremost and made the town an ideal place to raise your kids. The police were your friends and walked the street in plain view. We never locked our doors at night." Bill lent his take. "As a child, I went to the store one day for my parents to pick up some bread and butter. On my way home, I realized that I had lost a dime of my change. I quickly turned around to follow my tracks and ran directly into the storekeeper, who was trying to catch up to me to return the dime." Yes, times were simpler. So was transportation. As 1964 grad and athlete Pat Flynn described, "It was a farming community of 2,968 people. You could walk anywhere. I walked to school every day as I didn't have a car. None of us had cars in high school."

Dodgeville's history is as rich as its soil. The name derives from Henry Dodge, a Wisconsin senator from 1848 to 1857. Dodgeville for a time competed with nearby Mineral Point for the right to the county seat. Successful in this regard in 1861, the town housed the Iowa County seat in what is Wisconsin's oldest courthouse. In 1827, Dodge and a group of miners founded Dodgeville. He made a pact with the local Winnebago Indian tribe that allowed him to erect a small home and build a smelter. Originally, there were three settlements—Dodgeville, Dirty Hollow and Minersville. Dodgeville then became a village in the 1840s. It was not long before a population boom included a flood of miners from England—which explains the British architecture still conspicuous in the town. Indeed, with so many new residents Dodgeville soon found itself the biggest burg in Wisconsin and one of the largest in the Midwest. Such a run to greatness did not last long, however. The famous Blackhawk War, the even more famous California gold rush, and then the Civil War prompted a decline in the mining industry and a corresponding drop in population. Soon other centers like Milwaukee and Chicago came to eclipse Dodgeville. These events led to change and to the development of agriculture in Dodgeville. Because of its early settlements, downtown Dodgeville is one of Wisconsin's oldest districts. Historical buildings extend for a solid half mile down Iowa Street. But time does take its toll. Few of the shops and businesses of old have survived. Cherished exceptions include Nadler's A&W, the Singer Lumber Company, Bob's Electric, the Corner Hometown Pharmacy, the Quality Bakery, Arthur Real Estate, and the *Dodgeville Chronicle.*

Interesting is the role that each of these establishments plays in the dynamics of this book. Nadler's A&W was purchased by Merlin Nadler (married to Vicky Meuer, a 1964 grad) in 1962. Merlin had learned that the business was for sale from Coach John "Weenie" Wilson's sister, who was running the A&W in Lake Mills. Nadler's A&W has employed some 2,500 folks over the years. The site, at the north end of town, was a popular hub for the 1964 Dodgeville players. Nancy (Eichorst) Buck, the wife of longtime Dodgeville Hall of Fame coach Bob Buck, carhopped here in 1963 and 1964. A Dodgeville cheerleader during her freshman year, Nancy related, "I was a carhop my first summer and worked inside the next. It seemed to be the place to go and hang out for all of us at that age. As carhops we did not use skates but we did have to go out to the cars and take their orders and place them on the tray on the half-raised car windows."

Singer Lumber was founded over a half-century ago by current manager Tim Singer's father, Bill, now a 90-year-old lifetime resident. Bill's father Charles spent many years mining zinc and lead. Bob McNeill, who opened Bob's Electric in 1961, has served as president of the town's Chamber of Commerce. The Corner Home Town Pharmacy, run today by Larry Crowley, was once owned and operated by the Schill family. Daughter Donna Schill, a 1964 Dodgeville grad, was the prom queen her junior year along with king Bob Rock, a member of the Dodger basketball team. Donna was also a cheerleader in her days at Dodgeville. The Quality Bakery was started by LaVerne Crubaugh in 1928. It was taken over in 1949 by his son Mike, brother of 1963 Dodgeville Assistant Basketball Coach John Crubaugh. At age 15,

Mike ran the bakery, participated in football, basketball and baseball and became the valedictorian of his class. Currently the bakery is owned and operated by Brian Crubaugh, son of Mike. Arthur Real Estate has been a Dodgeville constant for over eighty years. Founded by T. Harry Arthur in 1929, his granddaughter is 1964 Dodgeville graduate Ginnie (Arthur) Helin. The business is currently owned by Jim and Patty Blabaum and called ERA Arthur Real Estate. Finally, the *Chronicle*, co-owned by Pat and Mike Reilly, has been in existence for over a century and a half. Published every Wednesday, the paper has a circulation of over 5,000 to serve Dodgeville and surrounding communities. Pat was a member of the 1963 state tournament basketball team, while brother Mike, as a freshman, was a team manager and wrote for the *Chronicle* in his last three years at school.

Victoria (Evans) Keyes is a 1970 Dodgeville graduate. Older brothers Ronnie (1954), Bradley (1958), and Gregory (1962) were multiple-sport Dodgers. All played under Coach Wilson. Vicki's husband, Jim (1966) was a football player. "Dodgeville is a great place to live," Vicki told me. "It's due mostly to the people—good, kind-hearted, hard-working folks who have many interests. Badgers, Packers, local sports teams, Governor Dodge State Park, close proximity to Madison, Dubuque, Chicago and Wisconsin Dells, to name a few—these afford residents a wide variety of opportunities."

Vicki's father, Daniel Evans, was a self-made man of many interests and talents. Born in 1913, he was a jack-of-all-trades—miner, farmer, hatchery manager, manager of a roofing company, restaurateur, campground owner, even a model for a professional photographer whose portraits won blue ribbons. Evans also published stories in several magazines and wrote five books. "Dad's books were all inspired in an effort to preserve history, historical places, traditions and old ways," says Vicki. "Dad had a great love of all and felt an obligation to capture it for future generations." His book, *Out of the Past*, described farm rituals such as butchering, sorghum-making, threshing, and home-partying. He went on to found the Iowa County Historical Society, an antique club and the Upland's Writers Club.

But of all of Evans' interests, his favorite was Hideaway Acres. In 1957, at season's end, the Dodger basketball team, who included Vicki's brother Bradley, was invited to the Evans home. Dan and wife Elaine served a meal fit for a king. "They ate every speck of food with relish," Vicki recalls. "Weenie Wilson and the team joked about how good everything was and suggested mom and dad should open a restaurant, and that is just what they did." The 238-acre farm the family had purchased in 1952 was a perfect site. "Dad was a doer and planner. Mom was the best cook/baker on the face of the earth—his perfect complement," says Vicki. In fall, 1958, without telling his wife, Evans placed an ad in the local paper. Folks responded, making the first official meal Thanksgiving dinner. Hideaway Acres, now officially open to all, became a Dodgeville landmark for home-cooking and family fun. "Time after time," says Vicki, "people who toured the House on the Rock and ate at the Hideaway remarked,

'I've already seen the House on the Rock, I just came back for the lemon pie!'"

Evans wanted to kick it up a notch. In 1963, at the suggestion of the manager of Governor Dodge State Park, Evans added campsites, shelters for the winter sledding parties, pony rides, trail rides, buggy and sleigh rides led by Belgium horses. There were hayrides, square dances, plays, and even a Sunday church service. There Vicki worked from 1964 until 1991, when they closed due to her father's cancer. In 1997 Vicki and spouse Jim bought the farmhouse and land from her mother to keep the memories alive. Today Vicki, Jim, brother Ron, and mother Elaine live there. Now 93, Elaine still bakes a mean lemon pie. Ron makes a nomad stew said to be as good as Daniel's. "My husband and I are the same kind of team as my parents," Vicki tells me. "We both love entertaining and sharing the magic of Hideaway. I sell perennials and have over fifty gardens. People don't have to pay anything to tour the gardens, but they must promise to enjoy them! We get so many comments about the warm, homey atmosphere of the house and grounds. That feeling is attributed to the many 'ghosts,' whose laughter, enjoyment and memories haunt Hideaway in a very good way."

Another vital factor in this story, perennially American, is education. By the early 1830s the area's first teacher, Robert Beyer, had arrived, asking parents to compensate him for providing an education for their children. The first schoolhouse, the "Old Rock School," greeted another teacher, Mary Carrier, who would wed a local and become

Mary Carrier Ranger. By mid-century the school had expanded and split into two districts. As our nation grew in curiosity and size, so did Dodgeville. Not long after the new century began, a new high school was constructed. Around 1940 another was built, followed by a third in 1962. In 1963 Ridgeway High and Dodgeville High consolidated and became one school. This would prove to be a pivotal year for the athletic programs. While Dodgeville High School serves students from both Dodgeville and Ridgeway, one elementary school is located in Dodgeville and the other elementary school in Ridgeway. St. Joseph's Catholic School serves students from kindergarten through eighth grade. Called the Dodgers (with a "D" for the team symbol), Dodgeville High teams play in the Southwestern Wisconsin league, with the Dodgeville-Mineral Point football game, dating back to the 1890s, one of the oldest rivalries in the state.

The value of education and athletics shows in prominent figures who hail from the area and is a tribute to the values the community holds so dear. Glen A. Abbey served as the U.S. consul in Salonika, Greece, in the 1950s. William Dyke, a two-term mayor of Madison, was the Independent Party's Vice-Presidential candidate in 1976, alongside Lester Maddox. Currently, Dyke works as the chief judge of the circuit court in Iowa County. Additionally, Stephen Hilgenberg, a Democrat, was a member of the Wisconsin State Assembly. He represented the 51st District and served from 2007-2011. He is also a former member of the Dodgeville School Board. Another Dodgeville native, Archie Hahn, one of the last century's top sprinters, ran for the University of Michigan. Hahn collected a trio of gold medals in the 1904 Olympics in St. Louis and one more two years later in Athens, Greece. Finally, there is Homer Fieldhouse, who created some five dozen golf courses across the Midwest.

Perhaps best known of all is architect Frank Lloyd Wright. Born in Richland Center, Wright designed over 1,000 structures. One of them, Taliesin, which means "Shining Brow," situated in nearby Spring Green, Wright built in 1911. There he resided for many years. Much in the spirit of Dodgeville, Wright emphasized the notion of human endeavor not opposing but harmonizing with nature. South of Taliesin sits the House on the Rock, a project completed by Alex Jordan after being started previously by his father. This tourist attraction opened to the public in the early '60s. Many believe that the house is a satire of Wright's work.

Even a summary as brief as this one exhibits the values of the tight-knit community that is Dodgeville, the heritage, and the legacy that has come and remains.

Most towns have a history of unusual events that occur. Dodgeville is no exception. In a very strange occurrence, during the winter of 2005, a kangaroo appeared, hopping around in the snow on farmland on the outskirts of town. News stations throughout the country, including the *Chicago Tribune* and MSNBC, carried the story. No one had any idea where the kangaroo had come from. Within a few days of its appearance, it was captured and transported to the Henry Vilas Zoo in Madison. To this day no one has any answer for this mystery. As of last count, the kangaroo is still at the zoo. With the Dodger passion for fitness and athletics, I wonder if anyone had alerted then-current basketball coach Chuck Tank, a 2010 inductee into the Wisconsin Basketball Coaches Association Hall of Fame, to a new resident in town with a tremendous leaping ability!

Mary Brown, the mother of 1964 Dodger basketball player Rick Brown, has lived in Dodgeville all of her ninety-three years. She taught at the high school for two years, then became the school's administrative secretary/treasurer for twenty-five additional years and worked for three successive administrators—Stan Anderson, Stan Orr, and Monte Hottmann.

I asked Mary about the advantages of living in Dodgeville. "Dodgeville is a good place to live. The people are outstanding," she told me. "For me it was a great place to raise a family. Everyone took an interest in each other's family and their care. The school system was first class. *All* the teachers made a point of knowing each child, of creating close relationships with their students." She told me about family camaraderie. "After every game, parents would gather at one of the homes to discuss the game and share snacks. One parent would give the player who scored the most points a case of Coke—which he would share with the team on the way home."

I queried longtime Dodgeville local Jayne Harrison, mother of 1964 basketball point guard Bruce Harrison, about raising a family and living here for so many years.

"Dodgeville has been a great place to live these 90 years. Our town has grown—new people and many areas have a lot of new residential homes. We had grandparents to love and visit. That was a plus for our sons, too. We had an excellent school system and great teachers." It all comes down to neighborliness. Jayne continued, "The people of Dodgeville are so friendly," she explained. "That's the beauty of a small town. When I go shopping I always meet someone to visit with and I still have many longtime friendships which I cherish. Our close friends call each other every day and check on each other. I still have siblings nearby and we stay in close touch."

Christine (Humbert) Harrison, a 1965 grad, was the girlfriend of player Bruce Harrison. Their budding romance began as far back as grade school when she and Bruce were part of Mrs. Gertrude Peterson's divided 3rd / 4th grade classroom. Later she found herself intrigued with Bruce after her first co-ed party in 5th grade. Chris offered this, "It was the beginning, the first tinge of interest in a boy—and he was cute." Chris and Bruce both have fond memories of growing up as their families vacationed together at Lake Wisconsin. They began to go steady when she was a sophomore and Bruce a junior. They have been together ever since, married for 47 years. Chris, now a Florida resident, told me about Dodgeville and her years there. "I grew up in a small town where everybody knew your family. People were friendly, quick to forgive and ready to help you when you really needed it. There wasn't a lot to do in town so we made up games, caught fireflies, practiced piano, basketball, or twirling the baton. We sat on our swing sets and shared stories. There came a time when the entire town and surrounding area came together to support a group of players who loved basketball and their coach. It was the Cinderella story all over again, and everyone was better for it."

Yet another, more contemporary voice I should mention is that of Terry Edwards, currently the branch manager at the local M&I bank. Not just a banker, Terry has been an active writer, having followed his passion after earning a major in mass communication and journalism at UW-LaCrosse. For a dozen years he wrote a column for the local United Methodist Church newsletter, words routinely situated on the newsletter's third page. When Terry decided to compile his columns as a collection offering warm, pleasant, folk-wisdom observations through the eyes of a small-town narrator, he did so in a book he titled *The Third Page*.

I had an opportunity to catch up with Terry and query him about his philosophy in a small Midwestern town and asked him to cite a few examples. Terry replied with the following:

"Growing up in Dodgeville, Wisconsin in the 1960s was small-town America at its finest. I still remember the population posted on the signs at the edge of town – 2,911. We were an agricultural community and farmers largely supported the local economy. Everyone got paid on Friday and made their way downtown to do their banking and shopping.

There was no fast food, just good diners on the main drag. There were no supermarkets, but three small markets. We had a wide variety of retail shops. The downtown area always seemed to be bustling with activity.

Dodgeville was also full of churches. There was an unwritten law that no non-church-related activities were scheduled on Wednesday nights or Sunday mornings. There was a large Roman Catholic Church with a grade school on the southeast side of town and many of the members lived near there. As kids, we were the 'Publics' (I guess for public school) and they were the 'Catholics.' But, there was no animosity, and it made it easy to choose sides when we got together for pick-up games.

Sports were our social and physical outlet. Most young boys participated in the youth softball program managed by a Dodgeville legend, Herb Harris. All of the coaches and umpires volunteered their services. Summer evenings playing ball at Centennial Park were magical. To end the season there were all-star games and fun night, in which we competed in games for the coveted prize – a Baby Ruth candy bar!

On weekends, high school sports were king. The 1960s were a golden era in high school sports for Dodgeville. Up until 1963, all Dodgeville students attended the same three-story brick school in the middle of town. As grade school students we would see the high school athletes with their letter jackets and sweaters, and dream of the days we would be like them."

In 1963, our President was John F. Kennedy, the Wisconsin Governor was John W. Reynolds, Jr. and the Mayor of Dodgeville was J. Clifford Olson. Alaska and Hawaii had joined the union only a few years before. The Pope was John XXIII. The sound of the Beatles, the Dave Clark Five, Elvis and the Beach Boys reverberated throughout the nation. Inventions such as microwaves, cell phones, skyping, personal computers, and flat screens were non-existent.

However, something more basic and much more significant did exist. Through the years the Dodgeville community had always had a core of residents who embraced faith, the work ethic, education and the family unit. These qualities and the climate they created furnished an environment ripe for success, for advancement whenever a challenge or opportunity loomed. One of these avenues of advancement was high school athletics. Here a special person with a strict, no-nonsense coaching philosophy — itself a reflection of this same setting, could perhaps hitch his wagon to these same precious values in order to make this community flourish and attain an additional sense of pride— "Dodgeville pride." Just as a farmer cultivates his crops in the early spring with hopes of great abundance, Coach John "Weenie" Wilson had been on a similar path since his arrival in 1944, encouraging these fundamental values in his players, integrating them into his system that in time would create a class of champions.

Even as the season drew to a close for the 1963-64 year, basketball was still on the minds of many in Dodgeville. The excitement and success of the Dodger team had never before reached such a heightened state of excitement. However, for many of the school's all-around student athletes, it was simply time to don another uniform and prepare for the next sport. The nucleus of the basketball team that had competed in Madison sent eight members to the baseball team and three to track.

Track-and-field was the venue chosen by Rick Brown, Bill Polkinghorn and Pat Flynn in which to spend their afternoons in the spring of 1963. They were coached by Joe Whitford. Brown chose to compete in the high jump and 440-yard run while Polkinghorn threw the shot put and discus and competed in the 440. Flynn participated in both the long jump and the high jump. (See the appendix for a complete listing of all team members.)

When Pat Reilly, Brian Olson, Duane Honerbaum, Corky Evans, Bruce Harrison, Dennis Morgan, Dave Johanning, and Bob Rock all eagerly showed up for baseball practice on day one, they were greeted by a familiar face—Coach Wilson. Coach Wilson had a vast sports knowledge as both player and coach.

Coach Wilson was a perfectionist, a huge believer in fundamentals no matter which sport was involved. He had a special knack of working well with the pitchers. Wilson had previously played minor league baseball and had been a teammate of Stan Musial in the Cardinal organization. When the spring weather was inclement, the team would take to the gym. The boys practiced hard. Fundamentals were emphasized on a regular basis. However, even Coach Wilson needed a little comic relief every once in a while. According to Dick Stephens, a sophomore and 1963 pitcher, one of those moments involved catcher and future minor-leaguer Corky Evans: "Corky had a younger brother named Joe who was pitching batting practice. Coach Wilson was watching from the stands behind home plate, and, when Corky came up to hit, Coach Wilson signaled Joe (without Corky knowing he was signaling to Joe) to throw up and tight to Cork. Joe, of course, followed what Coach was asking. Cork didn't appreciate Joe doing that, and after a couple of pitches, he swung and missed with the intent of throwing his bat directly back at Joe. Cork issued Joe a strong reprimand and to the rest of us, it was a funny situation. Cork didn't think it was funny."

Jim Meyers, head basketball and baseball coach from 1963-1974 at Darlington High School, went head-to-head with Wilson on a regular basis. He told me what transpired when the two schools met back in the day. "Years ago, the two teams who won the regional in baseball had to play a one game play-off to get to the sectional tournament. My first year coaching baseball in Darlington, we won the regional, as did Weenie, so we were to play. The two coaches were to meet and by the flip of a coin the home field was established. The day after the regional finals, I got a call from Coach Wilson. He said, 'Hi, Jim, congratulations on winning the

Regional. Now we have to flip a coin—we could meet at Dodge-Point Country Club and flip the coin there, but there is no reason for us to drive up there. How about having my wife flip the coin right here in our kitchen—you can call the flip, and get it done right now?' My response was, 'Weenie, you don't really think that I would agree to that?' He replied, 'Jim, don't you trust me?' I answered, 'Not any farther than I can throw a cow by the tail.' The best part is that for the next two years we were in the same situation, and, sure enough, he would call me and make me the same offer each year!"

Jim further offered this: "Coach Wilson's teams were always well prepared. His philosophy did not include a lot of flair. His teams were fundamentally sound. His kids were always tough outs. They put the ball in play and always put pressure on your defense."

Coming off a great season in 1962, in which the team had made it to the state tournament before bowing out to Beloit in the first round, the Dodger baseball team was again eager to start playing for real. The 1963 campaign, too, was to be a huge success. Once again winning the conference, the Dodgers finished the season with a 14-1 record. They again had made their way into the state tournament where they lost to Eau Claire Memorial, the defending state champions, in the opening round by a score of 5-0. Opposing pitcher, Jim Stewart, threw a brilliant one-hitter that included 16 strikeouts and three walks. Only first baseman Pat Reilly was able to manage a base hit in the fifth inning. Recently Stewart informed me he had really been up for that game against Dodgeville especially because of the one-point loss the Dodgers had pinned on Eau Claire in the state basketball tournament only a few months earlier. Stewart went on to the University of Minnesota on a baseball scholarship, deciding not to pursue any potential major league opportunities that were available. (See the appendix for a complete listing of all team members.)

Although no varsity basketball members went out for golf, Bob Anderson, Craig Brue, and Roger Perkins, all from the undefeated junior varsity team, would represent the hoopsters on the links in 1963. The golf team was only in its second year, having been added as a sport in 1962. Coached by Mr. Bomhoff, the team was originally comprised of four freshmen and two sophomores. Matches were held at the Dodge Point Golf Club, halfway between Dodgeville and Mineral Point. To compete against experienced programs like Richland Center, that in 1962 boasted two players who went on to compete at Division I schools, was no easy task. And there were other obstacles. "First, we had to teach coach Bomhoff how to play golf, as he had never played before," Mike Reilly told me. "The school didn't have transportation for us, so my teammate Roger Perkins drove us in his own car to matches. He usually drove 'a little over the speed limit,' *loved* to fly over hills to give us a thrill. We had great fun playing courses we couldn't normally afford. We also became good friends with those from other teams whom we would never have met if it weren't for the golf team starting up."

In 1963, its second season, the team won its first golf meet in school history, beating Lancaster and River Valley twice on a two-team-score basis. Craig Brue was medalist with a 40. Rounding out the scoring were Roger Perkins with a 43, Mike Collins with a 44, and John Nelson with a 46. Mike Reilly led Dodgeville's second team with a 41. (See the appendix for a complete listing of all team members.)

Soon came graduation day. It was time for the class of 1963 to bid farewell to Dodgeville High. It had been an incredible year, one never to be forgotten. The class of 1963 left on a very high note, proud of their many achievements. They would now say their final goodbye to Dodgeville High having an enormous sense of pride that would sustain them. The memories would last in time.

Summer was now in full swing. The smell of hay and fresh-cut grass permeated the air. Like other students, next season's returning basketball players were looking forward to a little summer fun, but each knew quite well he was expected to work. Corky Evans continued to work each day on the family dairy farm that provided three crops of hay. Other duties included sowing and harvesting, along with feeding the cattle herd each day. Dick Stephens mowed lawns and was a busboy with Larry Wagner at the new restaurant in town, Thym's Supper Club. Kramer Rock toiled on the family farm bailing hay and milking cows, while Bob Rock shoveled grain and ground up, mixed, picked up and delivered farmer's feeds for his father at Bob Rock and Sons Agricultural-Service. Tom Schleck was employed at the local A&W. Pat Flynn worked in a gas station. Curt Anderson worked on his father's carpentry crew. Rick Brown worked on the family farm with his brother. Mike Collins worked for his father in the plumbing business. Tom Brunker worked on the family farm and painted houses. Bruce Harrison worked at his Dad's Shell Station washing cars and pumping gas.

Although the boys worked all day, they honed their skills in basketball and baseball most evenings. Summer was a time to improve and overcome one's weaknesses. This notion was a given, as the Dodgeville athletes had been indoctrinated with this 24-7 work ethic from the time they were grade-schoolers and involved in youth sports. The players dedicated themselves to improving.

The introduction of youth programs in Dodgeville was instrumental in the city's sports success. The Babe Ruth baseball program, a national program with rules and regulations, was set up to allow teams to compete locally and ultimately advance to the national level. Referred to as junior Legion Baseball, it was the level of play prior to Legion ball. The emergence of this program in 1961 and the athletic prowess of the students of St. Joseph's Grade School helped strengthen youth sports in Dodgeville considerably. Volunteer coaches would donate long hours to the youth of Dodgeville, preparing them well for their transition to high school. These coaches were the true unsung heroes of Dodgeville athletics and its climb to the top. Dick Stephens, a 1964 team member described one such coach: "John Crubaugh is the unsung hero, in my opinion, for much of the success that Dodgeville had in both basketball and baseball during the 1960s," he told me. "He, along with Ralph Evans and Kenny Stephens, started the first Babe Ruth team that continues today. John's teaching and coaching of fundamentals was 'key' to our development in both sports. I think of John Crubaugh as the person who most influenced me as a player, as he was everything I thought a man was supposed to act like and play like. He was a great role model for all of us—tough, hard-working, kind, fun, and someone we believed in! I think he was the best coach I ever had in all of sports! As we advanced in age, our group continued by playing in the Legion program started by Am Morgan, a juvenile officer and the father of 1963 graduate Denny Morgan."

John Crubaugh also coached basketball for four years at Dodgeville St. Joseph Grade School, a popular alternative to the public school amid Dodgeville's large Catholic population. His teams practiced four times a week and played 25 games in a season. The other public school practiced much less and competed in under 10 games per year. To no surprise, John coached many of the 1963-64 players that went on to become great athletes at Dodgeville and was a natural to move up and assist Coach Wilson during the 1962-63 season. Because of this early affiliation with the players, he built a great rapport with all of them.

Mort Moyer, who followed Crubaugh at St. Joe's, amassed a record of 248-42. His teams had five practices a week and played many of their games on Sundays. In addition, they competed in numerous tournaments throughout the season. His 30-plus game schedule provided great experience for his players, who could then join the public school students as freshmen at Dodgeville. Mort Moyer also took over the Babe Ruth baseball program after Crubaugh. Offering basketball at St. Joe's, Babe Ruth baseball and then Legion play, was a distinct advantage for Dodgeville, compared to other high schools whose freshman students started school with a minimum of sports experience. The work of Crubaugh, Moyer, Ralph Evans and Kenny Stephens was vital to the success of Dodgeville basketball and baseball.

The 1963 Legion team, in a very competitive league, was coached by Ralph Evans, father of 1964 grad Corky Evans. The roster consisted of many of the same players from the spring high school team. The summer of 1963 saw their Legion opponents gunning for Dodgeville because the city had gone to state in both basketball and baseball the year before. The other teams wanted to set the record straight.

In most places in Dodgeville one could hear the bounce of a basketball. The sport had always been popular, but now, after being the state runner-up, the city had developed an insatiable thirst. Most families had a hoop at home. The City's Recreational Department had black-topped a new half-court at Centennial Park, a court some say Wilson had requested specifically as his team's very own practice facility. Kramer Rock, 1964 team member, described the summer action. "We scrimmaged unsupervised, of course. But, Harrison, Corky, Bobby Rock and others pretty much directed what we did.

We beat each other up pretty good in the lane, got blocked and pushed hard into the stupid pole holding up the basket and the backboard. No fancy-schmancy curved-out set-ups like today. This sucker was right vertical to the backboard. Stephens played hard, smacked butts and competed, raising the ability and intensity of all of us."

For at least three nights a week, team members showed up, both juniors and seniors. Juniors were welcome but would have to earn their place. Most of the seniors participated in that championship game and knew what it would take to repeat that scenario. There was a great deal of 3-on-3 play, but Wilson convinced some of the better local adult athletes to compete against his team. Many a night this provided for some brutal skirmishes, but the youthful Dodgers held their own. Player Bruce Harrison told me about some of those games. "A good friend and former Dodger, Tom Hughes, got all five of us together and brought in older guys to practice against us up at Centennial without Coach there. However, I did notice his car down the street, as he must have been watching us. I need to give Tom a shout-out here. I am especially grateful to Tom. He took me aside and helped me to learn how to become mentally tough and how to handle Coach."

Other nights, when not meeting at the park, the players worked on their own games at home, sometimes taking hundreds of shots in an evening. Corky Evan's father had built a concrete slab to store corn cobs in the winter. By May, when the corn was gone, they erected a basketball hoop on one side. Many times over the course of the summer the players gathered here to play at the suggestion of Coach Wilson. The players never talked about next year out loud or what their true purpose was, but Pat Flynn flat out told me: "We were dedicated to getting back to the state tournament."

To bring driver's education to Dodgeville and expand his own resume, Coach Wilson attended a class at UW-Platteville in the summer of 1963. Gari Walz, a biology teacher who had moved to Dodgeville in June, also enrolled in the same driver's education class. "The first day of class I heard a class member identify that he was from Dodgeville, so I introduced myself to him after class," Gari recalls. "Weenie was the first Dodgeville teacher I met. He told me of his days with the Packers, and we became good friends. He was very humorous, very interesting. Weenie inquired if I had ever coached. I told him I had coached one season of 7th and 8th-grade basketball at Soldiers Grove Junior High in 1960 while teaching science and math." Completing his Masters degree in 1968, Walz taught thirty-five years, all but three in Dodgeville. I asked Walz how he had done in his lone season as basketball coach. He replied, "We were 13-0 and that one season became my coaching career." Walz, a letter-winning high-jumper in track at Platteville, supported Dodgeville athletics by operating the scoreboard for football games, judging events at track meets and helping with crowd supervision at varsity basketball games.

Surprisingly, some people reported to me that Wilson was a bit flamboyant, especially in regards to his choice in cars. One story that I heard said that Coach Wilson owned a red, 1962 Chevy Impala convertible with red interior. This unusual car could not be missed in tiny Dodgeville as he drove around on summer weekends, surveying the city. Perhaps this story is not too far off base. Recently I bumped into Eric Hagerup who mentioned another of Wilson's cars. Eric, a 1954 Dodgeville graduate, played football and basketball under Wilson, and also ran track. A three-time state-champion sprinter, he recalled Wilson's car back in the 1950s and confided this somewhat amusing story. "Coach Wilson would drive around town in a yellow, four-door Studebaker with a tapered hood that matched its tapered trunk. You couldn't tell if the car was coming or going! We all referred to the vehicle as the 'two-row corn-picker'—but never, never to his face!"

Wilson, who also loved to play golf, would have former players chauffer him to nearby Mineral Point and caddy for him when he participated in the Elks outings. Afterward, he would play cards in the clubhouse for hours, joined by other local coaches such as Coach Martin from Darlington or Reeves from Platteville.

For the student-athletes, many summer evenings ended at the local A&W, a popular choice. But with Coach Wilson patrolling the streets at night and on the weekends, the players sometimes moved their social activities out of town. After all, summer wasn't all work and athletics. Many nights the players found their way to Governor Dodge State Park. Frequently accompanied by girlfriends, they could swim, listen to the sound of Leslie Gore's "It's My Party" or The Surfaris' "Wipe Out," and enjoy the rural ambiance of both Cox Hollow and Twin Valley Lakes. The cool water was a refreshing break from the humid Wisconsin summer. On weekends the Mineral Point Pavilions offered dancing to the music of local disk jockeys. Many from surrounding communities, including Dodgeville and Hollandale, would congregate here. It was reported that years earlier Lawrence Welk had played at the Pavilions. More recently Vilas Craig and the Vi Counts had made a visit featuring their popular new hit "Little Miss Brown Eyes."

On several occasions, the players decided to stay in town and go bowling. There were four lanes, located ideally beneath the Red Room Bar and Restaurant. The Dodge Theater also presented gripping films such as *Beach Party, The Pink Panther* and *The Great Escape.* Regardless of their activities in or out of town, it appeared that Wilson had either FBI or CIA connections. He seemed to know everything that occurred in spite of the players' efforts to conceal their activities and whereabouts!

In July of 1963, Dodgeville's new football coach Ray Heim moved to Dodgeville from Jefferson to take over the reins of the football program. Ray brought energy, excitement and strong public-relations skills with him. He would also be implementing a new wrestling program for the Dodgers. Heim was immediately greeted by nine senior players as he unloaded his furniture from the moving truck. He said the boys were extremely friendly from the get-go and even offered a needed hand. According to Heim, the seniors adamantly advised him, "Coach, we're not going to lose a single game this year." Heim responded with, "I admire your positive attitude and the fact that you seniors want to go 8-0 in your senior season." The players said back, "No, Coach, we are going to go undefeated all year long in football, basketball and baseball." It wasn't easy for Heim to replace Chuck Spies as football coach, especially with the defensive assistant, Wilson, still on campus. However, Heim credits Wilson for providing a climate of discipline and instilling a winning attitude at Dodgeville.

Early August football practice included tough two-a-day practices at the Dodgeville Athletic Field. Home games would be played at Centennial Park. Heim's assistants were Don Dalton, Jim Cook and Joe Whitford. With a new coach and a new system, the implementation process would take some time. Heim's team ran a Slot-T and featured a solid passing attack. Defensively, they ran the Oklahoma defense that alternated from a 5-2 to a 4-3, however, they did not do much stunting (linemen altering their path to the quarterback). Despite the new-fangled system, the players picked up their schemes quickly and were clicking by the first game.

The initial coin flip at Dodger home games involved some unusual choices. The first possession was important in regard to not only ball control and prevalent winds but also terrain: Incredibly, the playing field at Centennial Park ran slightly uphill.

Winning over a very tough Iowa-Grant team by a score of 13-6 to start the season was huge. The next challenge was with Darlington, a team with a great football tradition. The Dodgers, playing very well, won by a convincing 32-0 score. Defeating both Boscobel and Lancaster by considerable margins, they nipped a tough Cuba City team, 28-26. Victories over Mineral Point and Mt. Horeb left the team 7-0 with one game to play against a powerful Fennimore squad.

In the final game of the season Fennimore struck first going 55 yards in 14 plays. On the next series the Dodgers were held. After Fennimore took possession, the offensive effort was quickly countered by an interception by Dodger Dick Stephens at the Dodger 24-yard line. After an exchange of possessions, the Dodgers tied the score at 7-7 with Bob Rock going in on short yardage. The score remained tied until the fourth quarter. At the very end of the third period the Dodgers were set to punt against a severe wind. The old scoreboard did not show exactly how much time was left in the quarter. With Harrison hurt, Corky Evans had volunteered to do the punting. Heim explained what happened next. "I was screaming to Corky to hurry and punt the ball before we were penalized yardage. Oddly Corky seemed very cool and in charge under these circumstances. Unbeknown to me, he had already asked the referee exactly how much time was left in the quarter. There being only two seconds, Corky let the clock run out before he kicked, thus putting that nasty wind at the backs of the Dodgers. This clever move was followed by Evans' 56-yard punt, pinning Fennimore back on their 23-yard line."

On the next series, Fennimore's fourth-down punt was partially blocked, giving the Dodgers possession at the 12-yard line. Eventually, Evans took the ball in for the score, giving Dodgeville a 14-7 lead. Later in the quarter, Dodger Larry Wagner hit the Fennimore quarterback as he was attempting to pass, and the ball squirted right into the arms of teammate Bob Rundle, who raced 49 yards for the score and a 20-7 lead. Later, Fennimore countered with a score on a screen pass to make the score 20-14, but a late drive by Dodgeville left the Dodgers at Fennimore's 9-yard line as time expired.

The Dodgers' big victory over Fennimore would have a permanent effect on the Heim family. Coach's wife Betty gave birth to their fifth child, a beautiful baby girl, the Monday before the game. Stopping in at the hospital to offer congratulations, the players urged the proud parents to name their child 'Victoria' in honor of their upcoming victory. Betty, on hand for the contest, told me that, yes, their request was granted: The newest Heim addition, Karen Victoria, would always remember the origin of her middle name.

Dodgeville had finished the season 8-0, their first undefeated season ever. This they had accomplished under their first-year coach Ray Heim. Ray, a class individual, wrote the following letter to his team's parents following the season:

"Dear Parents,

I am very proud to have had the opportunity to work

with and coach your son during this most successful football season. He has worked hard and has made many personal sacrifices to enable us to have that necessary team condition and spirit which was responsible for our undefeated season and conference championship.

All of us cannot be champions. Only those who have God-given ability, desire, and a willingness to sacrifice and work toward their goal can achieve such a great honor. Your son has reached his goal on the football field. He has learned his lessons in football excellently, but there are other important attributes that he has learned as well. To name a few: self-discipline, competitiveness, ability to think under pressure, emotional control, humility in victory, perseverance and sportsmanship.

You, as parents, (especially you mothers) must also be commended for your aid during this past season. I know you have had added work such as washing his dirty football gear, watching what he ate before the game, helping him keep training rules, sympathizing with him when he was injured, consoling him when things did not go his way, etc. I sincerely want to thank you for your kind help and especially for entrusting your son to our care. As a father, I too can imagine what it must be like for you to see your boy get hit, pushed and driven to the ground and all you can do is sit there and hope and pray that the coach knows what he is doing and what he thinks best. You may be assured that the welfare of your son was always foremost in my mind.

God bless you and your son. May he always be a

tight end runs a button hook or a post player begs for the ball just above the block, each eagerly seals the defender with their body position. It is then up to their teammate, the quarterback or the perimeter player, to make that timely pass to their sweet spot.

Besides these learned habits, come a host of other benefits from playing multiple sports. A few include increasing stamina, developing teamwork, developing a winning attitude, not burning out in one sport, using touch, learning angles, being positive, sacrificing yourself for the betterment of the team, performing under pressure, developing sports intuition and of course, having more fun. These benefits strengthen trust, loyalty, respect and confidence.

Yes, the Dodgeville players were both multi-skilled and knew their teammates quite well. They played sports non-stop the year round and developed a strong chemistry. However, a final ingredient to the Dodgeville recipe of success was coaching leadership. Their mentor, Coach Wilson, had an all-around background as both a player and coach. As a high school senior he went to state in basketball, played football for the University of Wisconsin, the University of Dubuque, and for the Green Bay Packers. In addition, he played minor league baseball in the Cardinal organization. For many years he coached football, basketball and baseball at Dodgeville. He had a high-IQ sports mind. His ability to draw up a safety blitz, design a staggered double pick for an off guard, or explain the precise timing of a suicide squeeze could be done at moment's notice. When you went to battle, you wanted

Coach Wilson on your sideline, certainly not the other. He was a lethal technician whose game plan always packed a powerful punch. Opponents always knew they were in for a *game* against Dodgeville's John Wilson.

The way the sports seasons adjoin each other—the football season ending with the final Friday game and the following Monday bringing the first practice of the next seasonal sport, such was the case in 1963. Yes, by the time the leaves had turned colors and the last play from scrimmage had been run, everyone knew what lay just ahead. Could the Dodgers somehow find a way to recapture the marvel and pageantry of the last basketball season and once again taste success at the ultimate level? Yes, they had lost some great athletes from the 1963 state runner-up squad, but with a solid group returning and a summer of hard work and practice behind them, perhaps they felt they could. Only time would tell.

Chapter Four

Excitement and high expectations filled the air as the Dodgers took the floor for the first basketball practice. Based on last year's record of 23-2 and their strong nucleus returning, expectations were extremely high. Coach Wilson addressed the team and flat out told them they *could* win the state championship. To several others outside of his team, including some press members, he let his true feelings be known by announcing publically that his Dodgers *would* win in Madison. Wilson had tasted the excitement and pageantry of the tournament and now wanted another giant guzzle.

The new season would combine both the old and the new. A new school had been built for the 1963-64 school year. The new gym had a larger seating capacity of 800 seats, compared to 350 at the old school. The community hoped, however, that despite the new facility, the Dodgers would still maintain their old fashioned, hard-nosed approach.

Wilson and the Dodger squad would not disappoint them. I asked Kramer Rock what the old gym and the crowds were like. He was more than happy to address the question: "The gym, to use the expression, truly was a 'cracker box.' The out-of-bounds stripe was maybe a foot from the first bleacher. I remember students having to lift up their legs so the inbound player could even stand. There was an unusual game rule at the time. The defender had to stay at least three feet away so the in-bounding player could at least have a chance to pass. The scoreboard was archaic; the timer had a conventional moving hand and the scores were on a roll of paper and were advanced manually and often incorrectly. Not crowd-related info per se, but the shenanigans, bias and 'oops, sorry' errors by the home scorekeeper/timekeeper, both at home and away, often made even modest crowds sound like Madison Square Garden during a championship fight, with the yelling and screaming about clock errors. Wins beget awareness; awareness begets fans, fans beget rabid fans. As success (wins and losses) grew, so did attendance."

James (Joe) Whitford, an industrial-arts teacher, was Wilson's varsity assistant in addition to coaching the junior-varsity (B team). In the scheme of things, Joe played the good cop while Wilson's role was the bad cop. Whitford played a very critical role because the players were many times able to communicate with him on issues they felt they could not take to Wilson.

To get ready to compete for the season, the players would once again have to endure the "Wilson boot camp" from Day One. Coach Wilson looked up to Vince Lombardi, but many felt he far exceeded the famous Packer coach in terms of sheer toughness. He wanted his players to strive to improve and never back down in the face of adversity. Wilson's rules were the law, and he made it clear that his practices were not held for the players' enjoyment. Wilson felt that practices should be difficult both mentally and physically to ensure that games would be easier. He emphasized that whatever you do, do it to the best of your ability, day in and day out.

As 1964 team member Corky Evans states, "Our practices were so much more intense than the games. Coach Wilson made practices hell that way. He felt the mental approach to sports was equally as important as the physical approach. Coach felt that good practices will lead to good games. Coach was extremely intense and detailed. His practices were so organized and intense. There was absolutely no goofing off in practice. He told us goof-offs were not welcome."

Kramer Rock, a 1964 team member put it this way: "Wilson believed how you practiced was how you played. Slackers were ridden like a saddle." Players were confronted by Wilson in practice on a regular basis. Rock continued, "Often his spit was running off your nose. He controlled our destiny and we really wanted to be part of that team, so we did not quit." He went on to say, "If you didn't ask 'How high, Coach?' when he said jump, you were screwed. No one in my memory defied or questioned Wilson and played on his teams. I remember a couple that did, and they were banished."

Tom Brunker, a 1964 team member, was a transfer from Ridgeway High School one year earlier, where he had twelve students in his entire class. He had no idea what to expect at his first basketball practice under Wilson. "Being a transfer student to Dodgeville, after my first practice I was like 'numb.'" Even after a year of experience under Wilson the practices were no easier this year. For Wilson's practices, you had to be acutely ready, both mentally and physically.

Wilson's teams would fight and scramble for every loose ball. He loved to see this type of effort from his players, especially those willing to go to the floor without fear or apprehension. To help reduce their fears, Wilson not only furnished knee pads as part of the uniform, but required his entire Dodger team to wear them. This philosophy went back to his own high school days when he himself wore them. Many an opposing team got a chuckle when the Dodgers first took the floor, each fitted in his pads, but soon found out the Dodgers weren't only making a fashion statement, as they backed it up with their aggressive, unrelenting play. On most occasions the Dodgers were first to go to the floor.

Wilson did not allow his team to listen to music in the locker room, even though many other teams enjoyed this luxury. I asked '64 member Dick Stephens about any other unusual team rules instituted by Wilson. He replied, "We had a curfew rule, a hat rule, and a girlfriend rule (no holding hands in school). He would patrol Main Street on Wednesday night, church night, to make sure his boys weren't out past curfew and it was rumored that he was known to call your home. After a nice win, usually on the road, he would announce that 'The lid was off!' This meant that we could stay out until midnight instead of 11:30. This announcement to the team was very special for us because it signified he was pleased with us." Several other players reiterated that after practice you better not get caught without a stocking cap on. With many of the players wearing the new-fangled 'flat top' haircut, the hat rule seemed to defeat the purpose!

Randy Jackson (class of 1966), who played basketball, baseball, and cross-country for Wilson, told me, "Before the season players had to sign a two-page set of rules that Coach had drawn up. We and our parents had to promise to live by them. Also, Weenie had a ruler with a red mark on it. He would place the ruler atop the middle of your head and lift your hair. If your hair met the red mark, he would tell you: 'Get down to the local barber.'"

Alumna Dianne (Peterson) Mingione, 1963 homecoming queen and girlfriend of 1963 player Pat Reilly, gives us another glimpse of Wilson. "During the season the players would practice shooting free throws at lunch. We girls would sit in the bleachers, watching and eating our lunch. Coach Wilson would do his best to make sure the players did not engage in conversation with us. He also frowned on the players walking us to class or holding hands. As I lived in Edmund, some seven miles from Dodgeville, Coach would always tease Pat about going straight home after games and not taking any detours to Edmund."

Classmate Jeanne (Schmoekel) Paquin's father was the mayor of Dodgeville for seven terms, from 1968 to 1982. Jeanne, who was 1964 player Pat Flynn's girlfriend and future wife, said this of Wilson: "He had his hat rule that the guys absolutely hated. He would drive around, especially on weekends, looking for curfew-breakers. Yet he had a sense of humor and would always kid us girls. He was quirky, but we all knew he wanted the best for the boys. For this we respected him."

Christine (Humbert) Harrison, player Bruce Harrison's girlfriend and future wife, gave her take on Wilson and his ways in 1963. "Coach Wilson was very nice to me and all the kids. He would call me by name, say hi and visit for a minute or two ever so often. He was always around and we all accepted him and respected him. He would talk about the importance of getting an education, working hard, staying focused. But his basketball players were 'his' and they needed to practice, rest and stay away from the girls during the season. They also weren't allowed to ice-skate— it weakened their ankles, or so I was told. Coach would roam the halls to see if his players were talking to girls. He had eyes and ears in the community that told him if any of his players dawdled on the way home from Wednesday night church choir practice. Some of them did and paid the price for it, too. On the weekends after Friday night basketball games, we would meet up at the Huddle Restaurant, walk home and talk. Once Bruce got his driver's license, we dated on Saturday nights, and I'm sure Coach got a report on how late his boy got home. To me, Coach Wilson was a lovely, kind man. I never doubted his authority and I trusted him to always do the right thing."

Player Pat Flynn added this: "Coach Wilson did not have children, so we were his kids. He was a father figure to all of us. Excellent coach, strong disciplinarian, and very demanding. We used to laugh that he had eyes in the back of his head, because he seemed to know about everything we did on and off the court." I asked Pat if Wilson had any special nicknames for the players. He said, "I think I was the only one with a nickname and it was 'Jinx.' I got the nickname from my teammates because I was always getting caught by Coach breaking his rules. Like not wearing a hat in the winter, talking to girls in the school hallways, or being out after curfew. If a teammate was with me, he got the same punishment. Usually wind sprints at practice." I then asked Pat if Coach had any special phrases he used. "Yes," he replied. "The only one I remember is 'Flynn what are you doing?'"

Utterly serious about his rules, Wilson sometimes went to extremes to enforce them. National High School Coaches Association Hall of Fame coach Dick Rundle was a 1952 Dodgeville grad and a four-sport athlete who went on to have a stellar football coaching career at Monona Grove (165-50-3), winning two state titles. While at Monona Grove he also served as head baseball and golf coach. The legendary golfer Andy North competed under Coach Rundle. In addition, Dick, a member of the Wisconsin Football Coaches Association Hall of Fame, coached semi-pro football for ten years. He is currently the Executive Director Emeritus of the Wisconsin Football Coaches Association, having been the Executive Director from 1990-2011. Dick offered the following story from back in the day. "On the night of the homecoming bon fire, when the ceremony was over I loaded four guys and their girlfriends into my Dad's pickup truck. How did we do that? As we were leaving town, at the last stop sign I looked out and saw Coach following us. He pointed back to town and followed me until I had delivered all seven people home. He met with me the next day and told me he would check on me every night at 9:00 p.m. I was to be in the window at my house and to wave to him as he sat in the street in his car. He did that for a very long time, showing the need for discipline and a caring attitude on his part. The players were always the one thing important to the program. Everything else was window-dressing."

On a more serious note, Dick talked about the values he took from Wilson and how they affected his own coaching style. "Every day you learned something about the skills necessary to be successful. I am 78 years old and still, daily, use skills he taught me. Coach was a very intense individual that expected your very best in everything you did. Not having children of his own, all of his players became his family. He consequently became a second father to each of us. That was good as you spent more time with him than you probably did with your family. I believe I was the same in the way I presented the necessary intensity to be successful. That, along with a certain amount of intimidation and at the same time togetherness to create a family-style relationship, was a primary recognition of our sameness."

Harold Chappell, a 1951 grad, played football and basketball for Wilson and competed in track. He told me the following: "I remember playing a pre-season scrimmage in a basketball game against Linden, a small school 10 miles west of Dodgeville. They had a rather rotund teacher (who was hired to teach, but told 'You'll also have to coach basketball.') Unfortunately, he didn't know much about the game, and one of the senior players berated him for some action he took during the practice session. I remember feeling sorry for the man and couldn't believe he'd talk to his coach in that manner. To my surprise he had no response to his player, but Weenie Wilson did. There was some SERIOUS chewing on that student's posterior, and, if his pre-confrontation measurements were 40-32-36, when he walked out of that gym, they were reduced to 40-32-22."

Coach Bob Buck, Wilson's predecessor at Dodgeville says, "Wilson was a strict disciplinarian and a tremendous defensive coach. He controlled every move in and out of the gym. He was a great fundamentals coach. He was a yeller, but mostly when his team was ahead, to keep their heads in the game. He was calmer when his team was behind."

Mort Moyer graduated from Dodgeville in 1960. He played for Coach Wilson and went on to be a coach at St. Joseph's in Dodgeville. Mort scouted every game for Wilson during the 1963-64 season. He later became a successful high school coach at Orangeville High School in Illinois. He said of Wilson, "He was an excellent coach, fundamentals were so important. We had good discipline. He was like a father and always there for his players."

Ross Vivian is a U.S. Army Korean War Veteran and played under Wilson. Involved in football, basketball, baseball and track at Dodgeville, the 14-letter winner and 1950 grad remembers how excited his coach would become, especially as games came down to the wire. He told me, "In a close game with Platteville, we scored a basket with seconds to go and went ahead. Weenie jumped up. As I jumped up, he was coming down, and his elbow hit me on the head."

I asked Ross what happened next. He replied, "Someone fouled out and I had to go in and everyone was screaming that blood was streaming down my back." Ross later told me that Wilson apologized to him, but Ross quickly added, "We did win!"

Dodgeville teams worked on skills development and fundamentals on a daily basis under Wilson. Assistant Coach John Crubaugh stated, "Wilson did some picking and rolling against a man-to-man but also used the scissor-cut off the center most of the time at the top of the key. Against the zone, he insisted on overloading and stepping in after you had passed the ball. He also taught the perimeter players to hit the pivot with an inside pass, after making a player exchange on the outside." John echoed Wilson's famous words, "Don't hold the ball!"

They ran full-court 2-on-1 and 3-on-2 drills regularly. Details such as proper cuts, screening and ball fakes were often emphasized. They ran a patterned offense and had a few special plays ready at a moment's notice. They were able to "freelance," as Wilson called it, *only* if it worked. They shot free throws endlessly and ran countless wind sprints. Wilson teams would take the floor for each game prepared both physically and mentally, boasting a no-nonsense swagger of toughness.

The team constantly worked on defensive principles such as footwork and slides. Constantly putting pressure on the ball and not allowing penetration were the keys. The man-to-man was and always would be their bread and butter. Wilson preached, "Never let the offensive man take the baseline on you!" However, they did work on 1-2-2 and 2-1-2 zones, and put in additional time strengthening their 1-3-1 zone. Here they utilized a quick player running the baseline and placed the longer players at the wings, allowing them to cover the corners and secure great rebounding position. The defender in the middle, usually the center, would be playing either in front or behind the opposing center depending on that opponent's size and ability. At the top, the point defender would trap on the wing to where the foul line extends or play the passing lane and make the opponent throw high lob passes from side to side, thus utilizing air time for each team member to adjust defensively.

Because of the popularity of basketball and success of the Dodgeville teams, the crowds for the games were massive. In the smaller gym the previous year, they actually had put planks on top of cement blocks to add more seating. The new gym offered more seating, but regardless, it still wasn't nearly enough. Just as they had done the year before, they again had to make accommodations for the huge crowds. The band once again played for the pre-game and for half-time from the stage at one end of the gym. Once they were through playing, more chairs were quickly added. With standing-room-only crowds for almost every game, they were later forced to set up a closed-circuit TV monitor in the lunch room to accommodate the overflow crowd. Without a doubt, Dodgeville usually brought more fans with them for away games than the home teams turned out.

Dodgeville: Capturing Hearts

The game ritual was always the same. As 1964 player Dick Stephens tells, "The team would arrive individually at the gym to watch the JV game. At the end of the third quarter, we would leave as a unit to go get dressed. When the team got up to get dressed, the students and fans would applaud. The acknowledgement of the 'Varsity Team' going to get ready was understood by all. We had great support." In the locker room, per Wilson, the team was to keep its mind strictly on the game. As the varsity finally made their way to the floor for warm-ups the crowd went crazy. The band performed several songs, with "When The Saints Come Marching In" being a customary tune.

When the team warmed up before a game, Wilson expected warm-ups to be fundamentally sound and not include the least bit of "hot dogging" as he felt that this behavior would lead to lack of concentration during the game. Bob Rock told about Wilson and the one time the team pushed the envelope. "He felt strongly about not grandstanding and not showing off. There was one time (and only one time) that we were doing a little too much 'globe-trotter' ball passing during pre-warm ups. The crap hit the fan and he ran over to our little circle and chewed our asses so everyone in the stands could hear/see it (Dodgeville home game). Though embarrassed, we smiled to ourselves (inside), toned down our warm-up routine—and knew he was right."

The season would open away, against Platteville. Being superstitious, Corky Evans had made the trip wearing his red tie and red socks, his signature look. He would wear this combination every game of the year for good luck. Wilson was very strict about concentrating only on the opponent at hand and not looking ahead. He always felt that the ball should initially go inside on offense, which was built around their big horse, pivot player Rick Brown.

Wilson had pointed to the Platteville game since early summer. With a large crowd on hand, the season began with every bit of excitement it had ended on in the prior year. Before the Dodgers took the floor, Wilson had asked last year's captain, Pat Reilly, to address the team. Pat remembers this well, "He invited me to the locker room at Platteville the next year to speak to the team before the game. He didn't have to do that, but I will always be glad he did. I loved playing with all those guys in 1963 and cheering for them in 1964."

One interesting fact is that during the 1961-62 season the five starters for this 1963-64 season had been moved up to varsity by Wilson when they were sophomores. They did not play much in the games, but were able to go head-to-head with the starters every day. I asked 1964 starter Bob Rock the result of this move by Wilson. He stated, "I remember during those practices how hard we tried to out-do, out-rebound and out-run the first team. I remember times that Weenie chewed some royal butt because we showed them up (on occasion) during practice. The pride was forming."

Wilson had put the season's objectives on paper for his team on Day One. The first objective was to take care of Platteville, the second to win the league and the third to win state. Wilson's starters would be Rick Brown, Corky Evans, Pat Flynn, Bob Rock and Bruce Harrison. Starting center Rick Brown was a muscular 6'5" and could run the floor like a deer. Forward Corky Evans was strong and brutal on the boards, yet he possessed a soft shooting touch. Forward Pat Flynn was a steady scorer and smooth as silk both inside and out. Bob Rock, a great all-around athlete, played the off-guard position and was valuable under pressure. Finally, Bruce Harrison, as in football, was the 'quarterback' of the team. An honor student who would graduate 3rd in his class, Harrison was truly an extension of Wilson on the floor. The other 13 team members were extremely valuable. Many could have started on other teams. They provided fierce competition for the starting five in practice each and every day, making sure the starters earned their spots. These members included Tom Brunker, Mike Collins, Curt Anderson, Bill Harris, Craig Brue, Mike Gust, Kramer Rock, Danny Stombaugh, Tom Schleck, Larry Wagner, Ken Johanning, Steve Schroeder and Dick Stephens. The team managers were Bob Anderson and Bob Campbell. Wilson, a master technician, even had his bench players sit nearest to him in their normal substitution patterns. He would leave nothing to chance, even a timely substitution was well thought out. With every element now in place—players, coach, strategy, passion—it was finally time for the initial jump ball and the start of the 1963-64 basketball season. (See the appendix for a complete listing of all team members.)

Chapter Five

On Tuesday, November 19, the season was finally underway. The Dodgers were ready to play right from the start. Picking up where they had left off from their undefeated football season, they jumped all over Platteville from the opening tip. They raced to a first quarter lead of 23-14 and expanded it to 39-24 by half-time. The Dodgers were playing superbly at both ends of the court. Continuing their outstanding play in the second half, they increased their lead before substituting freely. The final score was Dodgeville 72 and Platteville 41. Rick Brown led the scoring with 18 points, Bob Rock added 15, Pat Flynn 12 and Corky Evans chipped in 10. For the Dodgers it was good to start out with a big victory and leave those first-game jitters behind.

Friday, November 22, 1963, was a day most Americans would never forget. It was the day that our President of the United States, John Fitzgerald Kennedy was assassinated in Dallas, Texas. Most people today can still remember where they were when they heard the devastating news that stunned our communities nationwide. Lyndon Banes Johnson, the Vice President was then sworn in as our new Commander-in-Chief. On Monday, November 25, all Wisconsin schools would be closed. Dodgeville's scheduled game with Lancaster would be postponed to a later date.

Despite the tragedy, many teams played their scheduled Friday games, Dodgeville included. Over 1000 people were on hand for the Dodger home opener. They would host Prairie du Chien, in the very first game to be played in their new gymnasium. The visitors resided on the banks of the Mississippi, only a bridge's distance across the mighty river from Iowa. Again the Dodgers jumped to a huge lead with their outstanding play, scoring the first 11 points of the game with Rick Brown scoring 5 and baskets by Bob Rock, Corky Evans and Bruce Harrison. The Blackhawks could do little to stop the onslaught. The Dodgers turned a 27-4 first-quarter lead into a margin of 46-18 by half-time. The Dodgeville starters played only about half the game, but the Dodger bench continued to play aggressively. The starters accounted for 63 points as Flynn scored 22 and Brown added 17. Coming off the bench, Curt Anderson added 9 points while Ken Johanning added 8. The final tally was Dodgeville 97 and Prairie du Chien 41.

One-sided games such as this gave substitutes ample time to play. However, in order to play, Wilson had one more requirement. Team member Mike Collins told me the following: "I do remember that when we would get far enough ahead and substitutions were starting that he (Wilson) would get up and walk down along the bench. He wouldn't just look at us but would look into our eyes. I got a sense that if my eyes were conveying "I'm ready, I want to play," he would put you in. One time I wasn't, and he didn't."

Boscobel was the next opponent on the schedule. The Dodgers started slowly, unable to produce a scoring punch. Behind 13-12 at the quarter, they improved their offense in the second-quarter due to the solid play of Evans, Brown and Flynn. However, they allowed the Bulldogs 21 second-quarter points of their own before taking a 41-34 lead into the half. In the second half, the Dodgers finally got rolling, outscoring the Bulldogs by a 48-24 margin. For the evening Pat Flynn and Corky Evans each scored 24 points to lead the Dodger scorers in the 89-58 victory. With the victory, the Dodgers were now 3-0 for the season and held a one-half-game lead over arch-rival Iowa-Grant.

Next up for the Dodgers was the makeup game against Lancaster, rescheduled because of the death of President Kennedy. When we think about the importance of the Dodgeville - Lancaster rivalry through the years, we need not look any further back than last season's finale. It was the Dodger victory in a triple overtime, slow-down barn-burner in the first game of the state tournament that was still on everyone's mind. It was a victory that allowed the Dodgers to continue their march to last year's state finals. Not only had the game been close, but it upset Coach Wilson quite a bit. Lancaster had slowed down the game, thinking this would be their best chance to stay close to the talented Dodgers. After the game, Wilson was visibly upset and paid a visit to the opposing locker room. He barged in and found Coach Paulin in the coaches office a few feet from his players who were dressing. Wilson had pointed his finger at Paulin and said, "Anyone that stalls against my team would be remembered." A surprised Paulin told me what had happened next. "I said, 'Weenie, are you threatening me?' He said, 'No, not you, but anyone else that stalls against us.'" John added, "Weenie had an ego, but he deserved to have one. He was a great coach, and you always had to look beyond what he was saying to make an assessment of him." He told me that playing against Wilson's Dodgers was no easy task. "You didn't expect too many surprises, but you had to concentrate on playing good sound basketball to expect to stay with him. His players were so well drilled that they expected to run the same play over and over again until they got it right."

From the start Lancaster came ready to play. Defensively prepared, they did not allow the Dodgers to pass the ball inside to big man Rick Brown. Consequently, cold outside shooting by the Dodgers produced another sluggish first half. The Arrows first quarter lead of 15-12 was still intact 23-21 at half-time. But again the Dodgers came alive in the second half, outscoring the Arrows by a 34-21 margin with Pat Flynn leading the way scoring 20 points for the evening and Bruce Harrison adding 13. Keith Jerret paced Lancaster with 15. The final score was Dodgeville 55 and Lancaster 44. Thus far, Lancaster had been the Dodgers' stiffest competition. The Dodger record now stood at 4-0 for the season.

Next up was Fennimore. The Dodgers came out ready to play right from the beginning. With Rick Brown scoring with ease inside, their 20-14 first quarter lead grew to 42-23 by half-time. Clicking on all cylinders, the Dodgers expanded their lead to 74-48 before substituting freely. The final score was Dodgeville 87 and Fennimore 61. Brown ended the night with 28 points while Pat Flynn and Bob Rock added 18 and 15 points respectively. Clayton Wood led the Eagles with 19 points.

Dodgeville was on its game as they hosted West Grant the following Friday. It would prove to be a record evening for the Dodgers. With pressure defense and fast-break basketball, the Dodgers took a commanding lead of 23-8 at the quarter and pushed the margin to 46-23 at half-time. The onslaught continued in the second half as the Dodgers put up 36 in the final period. Dodgeville's Pat Flynn took scoring honors with 32 points on the evening. Corky Evans added 21 and Rick Brown chipped in 19. Dick Stephens' two free throws late in the fourth period brought the Dodger total for the evening to 99 points. Then Flynn's replacement, Kramer Rock, hit a long jumper from the side giving the Dodgers points 100 and 101. The final score was Dodgeville 103, West Grant 44. The 103 points was a gym record eclipsing the 97 scored against Prairie du Chien weeks earlier. We must realize that this Dodger scoring feat was achieved before the debut of the 3-point shot in Wisconsin high school basketball (1987), which accentuates the achievement even more.

The Dodgeville team was now undefeated at 6-0 as they went into Christmas break. They held a one-game lead over Platteville in the Southwestern Wisconsin League.

One hot-spot in downtown Dodgeville, especially on Saturdays, was Kip's Barber Shop. A red-and-white pole adorned the front of the shop where owner Kip Olson and co-workers Maury Althaus and Vern Ott would cut hair. Years earlier barbers had performed surgery at this place of business, thus the red-and-white pattern signified blood and bandages. During the basketball season a substantial number of the town's male population would routinely congregate at Kip's to discuss in depth the previous night's game. These folks not only loved basketball but understood its most intricate workings. More than anything, they wanted to analyze the recent game's every detail. When Coach Wilson showed up (which he did often) it was a special treat. Everyone wanted answers, and Wilson was more than willing to oblige. Ott, still an active barber today at age seventy-three, told me what happened one day as he cut Wilson's hair. One of his customers came into the shop very excited. The customer's wife had just had a baby—after five boys they finally had a girl. Ecstatic, he handed Coach Wilson and Ott a cigar. The coach gave him a stern look. "When I get out of here, I'll head on over to school and get a collection going to buy you a TV," he told him. "Apparently you need something else to do at night!"

Coming back after Christmas break is always worrisome for a successful team. You hope that you can somehow get back into that same groove quickly. So it was with the Dodgers as they faced the Cubans on January 10, 1964 in Cuba City. Cuba City, a very tough team at home, was determined to give the Dodgers their first loss. In addition, the previous year's assistant coach, John Crubaugh, was now the Cuban's head coach and was very familiar with the Dodger team. In preparation for the Cubans and their high scorer, Gary Olson, Wilson needed a stand-in. Tom Brunker, 1964 team member remembers Wilson's request: "Weenie told me to be Gary Olson in practice (against the first team), he told me to shoot from anywhere during the scrimmage."

Early in the first quarter two buckets by Corky Evans and a three-point play by Bruce Harrison put the Dodgers up 7-2. The Cubans could never recover. By half-time the Dodgers held a commanding lead of 41-25. With Brown working the inside and Flynn the outside, the Dodgers seemed to be playing at their highest level of the season. Cuba City's Gary Olson, the league's leading scorer, scored 10 points in the first half. Corky Evans held Olson to 4 third-quarter points, and he went scoreless in the fourth. At the same time, the Dodger scoring continued for 35 second-half points. The final score was Dodgeville 76 and Cuba City 49. Rick Brown led all scorers with 29 points and Pat Flynn added 20. For the evening the Cuban's Gary Olson scored 14.

The next two games were played in Dodgeville. The first of which had the Dodgers hosting Mt. Horeb on January 17. In the first quarter, Mt. Horeb held its own, leaving the Dodgers up only by two at 17-15. In the second quarter the Dodgers exploded for 31 points and at the same time held Mt. Horeb to 12. However, at the end of the second quarter Pat Flynn ended up in foul trouble and was used sparingly in the second half. Taking his place was Curt Anderson, who came through with flying colors, scoring 11 points. The Dodgers continued their surge in the second half outscoring Mt. Horeb 42-26. The final score was Dodgeville 90 and Mt. Horeb 53. Rick Brown led the Dodgers with 22 points. Bob Rock added 17 and Pat Flynn added 16.

On many nights post-game dances were held in the

school cafeteria. The cheerleaders would announce the event during the game and would invite students from the opposing school. It was here that student Mike Riley, more often than not, would show up with his stack of the latest 45s and perform as the disk jockey. The entire team would attend, keeping a very sharp eye on Wilson's curfew requirement.

On January 18, the second game of the two-game home stand featured archrival Iowa-Grant. The Dodgers started the game slowly, and were down 5-1. With four minutes gone in the first period, a free throw by Corky Evans gave the Dodgers their first lead at 6-5. From that point, Dodgeville went on a tear, outscoring the Panthers 37-10 to take a commanding 43-15 half-time lead. The Dodgers maintained their lead in the third period and expanded it in the fourth. The final score was Dodgeville 88 and Iowa-Grant 44. Ten players were in the scoring column for the Dodgers led by Pat Flynn with 25 and Rick Brown with 21. At 9-0 the Dodgers were playing inspired basketball.

Being so close in proximity, Dodgeville and Mineral Point, had become natural rivals. Besides this, Dodgeville had been chosen over Mineral Point back in 1861 for the right to the county seat. This may not have been on the mind of the current Pointers, but none the less they were determined to give the Dodgers a game. Dodgeville jumped to an 8-0 lead with two baskets from Bob Rock and one each from Evans and Brown. The Dodgers never relented, as they built a 26-7 first-quarter lead and a half-time margin of 46-20. In the third quarter the Dodgers outscored the Pointers 21-8

Dodgers set a new single-game scoring mark besting the 103 points against West Grant.

The following Friday the Dodgers traveled to Mt. Horeb, feeling that competition might be a little tougher on the road. The 90-53 victory in Dodgeville would not soon be forgotten by the host Vikings. Right from the start, Mt. Horeb came out in a stall, holding the ball as seconds ticked away. Initially the score stood at 4-4 before pressure defense and a superior shooting display gradually took over for the Dodgers. Dodgeville led by 5 at the quarter, and 21-14 at half. But the lengthy possessions of the Vikings kept the game reasonably close and it was still a 7 point game after three periods of play. In the final period and behind by 8, the Vikings were forced to foul. The Dodgers responded with several free throws, winning by a margin of 45-33. Rick Brown led Dodgeville with 14 points and Pat Flynn added 10.

February 9, 1964 brought the dedication of the new high school. The Dodgeville High Band played before the program started. The president of the School Board, Robert Campbell welcomed everyone. Student Council President Bob Rock told the audience how much students valued the new facility. The dedication address was given by Jenkin Lloyd Jones, editor of the *Tulsa Tribune*. The theme of his address was the "Explosion of Knowledge."

Soon Dodgeville hit the road for a contest against the Panthers of Iowa-Grant. Again starting sluggishly, the Dodgers trailed after 4 minutes, 10-4. Iowa-Grant must have heard from Mt. Horeb the benefit of holding the ball and employed a semi-stall offense of its own. With the Panthers continually holding the ball, Dodgeville had to work hard to come back and finally took a lead of 17-15 at the quarter. The Dodger defense now took over, allowing the opponent only 6 points in the second period while scoring 17 of their own. Dodgeville now in control of the game, maintained a 43-27 lead after three periods. With the game getting chippy, a Panther player threw a body block on Dodgeville's Pat Flynn, sending him to the floor and then to the free throw line. The Dodgers responded and finished with a flurry and a 60-36 victory. Rick Brown led the Dodgers with 16 points. Bruce Harrison added 14 and Pat Flynn 12. Gary Lindauer led the Panthers with 21. With the victory, the Dodgers moved up to number three in the WIAA's Big 16 ranking.

Next up was a rematch with Cuba City and once again former assistant coach Crubaugh. Baskets by Corky Evans and Bob Rock gave the Dodgers an early 4-0 lead. With each team putting its defensive emphasis on the other's leading scorers, Flynn for the Dodgers and Olson for the Cubans, it was up to their teammates to take up the slack. The Dodgers rallied with a nine-point run just before half, giving them a 34-17 lead at the intermission. With the Dodgers hitting their shots, they continued to build their lead. Corky Evans and Curt Anderson held high scoring Olson to only 5 baskets for the evening, although he managed 9 free throws. For the evening the Dodgers shot 51 percent from the floor on 24 of 47 attempts in the 69-37 victory. Rick Brown led Dodgeville with 22 points and Bob Rock added 13. Gary Olson led the Cubans with 19.

Many a referee at Dodgeville had been subject to Wilson's scrutiny. Long-time referee Otto Puls often called games at Coach Wilson's venue. He recalled one game in the early 1960s and offered this twist. "On our arrival, my partner and I were ushered into the Dodgeville coach's office to dress. At that time coaches were given cards by the WIAA to rate refs on a scale of 1 to 10, with 10 being the highest rating. A solid rating allowed a ref to work regional and sectional games later in the season. While dressing, we noticed our cards sitting on the desk, already filled out. Each of us had received a 10 for the evening. Was this a ploy by Wilson for favorable treatment? We both thought about it—and both got a big laugh."

On February 15, Dodgeville would play a non-conference game against Lodi, a member of the Madison Suburban League. It was also the evening chosen for the dedication of the new gymnasium. Tied for the lead in their conference, Lodi came into the game with a 13-1 record. The first half was close, with both teams scoring readily and Dodgeville held a 41-33 lead at the break. Once again the third quarter was the turning point, with the Dodgers exploding for 35 points to Lodi's 9. With a 76-42 lead at the end of three quarters, the Dodgers subbed wholesale. The final score was 92-62. Rick Brown led the Dodgers with 31 points, Bob Rock had 19 and Bruce Harrison added 15. Bill Schilling led Lodi with 28. Dodgeville, shooting over 59 percent from the floor in the second half, was now 15-0 for the season.

In a rematch with Mineral Point on Friday, February 21, the Dodgers were ready right from the opening tip. Apparently the competition for the county seat was still on *their* minds. It was not until over 7 minutes had passed that the Pointers scored their first field goal. Dodgeville's suffocating defense was too much. At half-time, Dodgeville had a staggering lead of 31-6. The Dodgers continued to apply pressure in the second half and outscored Mineral Point 46-18 to earn the victory. The final score was Dodgeville 77 and Mineral Point 24. Rick Brown and Pat Flynn led the Dodgers with 23 and 22 points respectively. Bob Rock added 10 while Curt Anderson scored 6. The Dodgers had handled Mineral Point by big margins in both games. However, in two years' time the game would become somewhat tighter with their neighbor. In 1967, Mineral Point would hire a new upstart coach for one year who was destined for greatness. He would be confident and make it known that he knew just how to beat Wilson and his match-up zone. This in itself would infuriate Wilson and heighten the rivalry. The score of the game held at Mineral Point in 1967 was Dodgeville 46 and Mineral Point 42. Who was this new coach that would bring a breath of confidence to the Pointer program for one year? Dick Bennett, who would later coach at UW-Stevens Point, UW-Green Bay, UW-Madison and Washington State.

Only one game at Darlington remained in the regular season. With the game expected to be a sellout, officials at Darlington were warning that Dodgeville adults could not be promised attendance. Darlington had to take care of its students and their regular-season ticket-holders ahead of everyone else.

Throughout the season Wilson continued his iron diligence regarding curfew. For some players, breaking curfew and getting away with it was an exhilarating feeling. "I enjoyed the friendship and emotions of my first love, but as I age I find my getting away with flouting Coach Wilson's dictates of that time very satisfying as well," Kramer Rock explains. "He mandated time curfews. You'd swear Wilson never slept. If a team member was found to be out after the curfew on a weekend or during the week, Coach was in his face about it the next day. In a small town, the cops knew who drove what car. Zoom the family car around town at one in the morning and bang!—Wilson heard about it," he says. "Risking his wrath—or worse yet, risking getting kicked off the team—kept us in check. Well, kind of. Kept us *creative* is a better term. Being a teenager and getting around authority was as intertwined as date night and having a big zit show up on your cheek."

As for Kramer's first love, it happened this way. A 4-H member, in the summer of 1963 he exhibited his purebred dairy cattle at the Iowa County Fair. There by chance he met a young beauty from Darlington whose family raised purebred sheep. Rock fell head-over-heels. "She was cute, sweet, bright, outgoing," he recalls, "a kind of farm girl—a perfect match for a farm boy." But her most important virtue, he says, was her willingness to talk to him. The two struck up a chat and discussed common interests. "I was a scrawny little guy, as sophisticated as a gravel road," he tells of it. "But a month earlier, I had turned sixteen and gotten my driver's license. It was my passport to freedom and then to Darlington. Wow! The world *was* my oyster!"

Kramer had one distinct advantage over his teammates. His farm was on the southern edge of Dodgeville, and Darlington was twenty miles farther south. What's more, Kramer's parents gave him broad latitude as long as he didn't mess up. Generally, he kept his own hours, but he knew he better be up come chore time. With minimal sleep, he still woke each day for the 5:30 milking and chores. The late-night trips home from Darlington found him often swerving to avoid deer along Highway 23. *Did* Coach ever find out? "The cool thing is that I never got called out by Wilson for curfew. Never," he reports. "Living where I did and coming into town from the south afforded me cover from cops, snitches, and Wilson clones."

However, being Catholic and carrying around this form of untruthfulness did make Saturday nights at the confessional a bit difficult. Rock says he often wondered if fifty Our Fathers, fifty Hail Marys, and fifty Glory Bes was the penance *everyone* got.

Next up for Rock and the Dodgers would be Darlington, with Rock's girlfriend—a Darlington cheerleader, no less—in the house. He would have to make a concerted effort to maintain his game face and keep his eyes on the court. On Friday, February 28, the Dodgers arrived in Darlington. A season of hard work was on the line, and they wanted to end regular play with an unblemished record. Once again the Dodgers started strong, taking a commanding 19-10 lead. But the Redbirds came back strong in the second quarter, scoring 22 points. The Dodgers countered with 25 of their own to give them a 44-32 lead at the intermission. With each Dodger starter scoring in double figures for the evening, the lead reached 68-46 at the end of three periods. Clearing their bench, the Dodgers continued to score with Kramer Rock adding 8 and Tom Brunker 4. The final score, 107-69, was another season high for Dodgeville. Mike Gust's two free throws gave the Dodgers their final points. Flynn, Brown, Evans, Harrison and Bob Rock scored 23, 21, 21, 14 and 12 points respectively. Osterday led the Redbirds with 22. For the record, Kramer Rock did concentrate on the game, although he cast a few glances towards the Darlington cheerleaders.

The Dodgers had finished the season with a perfect record, a first for the school. In the seventeen games played, their margin of victory was a staggering 35.6 points. Some thought the team hadn't been truly tested during the regular season. However, expectations were high as the next critical step, the state tournament, drew near. At 17-0 the Dodgers were confident, but they knew they had only scratched the surface. A mighty challenge lay on the horizon.

Chapter Six

As tournament pairings were announced for the 1963-64 season, I began to get excited all over again. I had done my best to follow the Dodgeville team each week, poring through our newspaper in hopes of finding their scores. I hadn't seen every one, but every game I did uncover was a victory. Now with the brackets made public, I could trace the Dodgers path towards Madison. It had been so exciting the previous year that I remember praying that they would again make it to state. Most all my friends, too, were Dodgeville fans, even though our town of Delafield was located a mere ten miles from Waukesha, our obvious second choice.

As with every state tournament, there are always favorites. Waukesha was coming off a dismal showing in the month of February, dropping all the way to fourth place in the always-tough Milwaukee Suburban Conference. It would take a miracle run for Waukesha to join the field of eight in Madison. Milwaukee North and Racine Horlick had been mentioned as contenders for the state title and tiny Dodgeville was said to be a long shot, even though they were currently undefeated and actually ranked second in the Big 16 Rating behind undefeated Kenosha. However, many felt the Dodgers had not played a difficult schedule and had lived a banner year the previous season with little chance of repeating that aspiration.

Dodgeville High and the whole community were still on an emotional high. The 1963 season had brought new meaning to basketball with the acclaim they received from their second place finish at state. With this year's team presently undefeated and already being mentioned in the same context as North and Horlick, excitement was brewing in the air. Another run at the title was the foremost thought on everyone's minds. The Dodger's Corky Evans, a longtime New London, Wisconsin resident, told me, "Coach got a taste of the big time and he wanted back to the state tournament. Plus, we as players wanted back. We saw that we could compete with the big boys."

The pairings were announced over the weekend. Platteville was scheduled to be Dodgeville's first opponent. Prior to the game, starting forward Pat Flynn was interviewed by the school newspaper, the *Dodger Highlife*. He told why he was proud to be a member of the '63-'64 team. He cited Coach Wilson as a great coach and friend. He pointed out the unselfishness of his teammates, who are all are such good friends and have "one continuous blast together." He credited the cheerleaders for never losing their enthusiasm and the fans for following the team everywhere. He closed with, "How can anyone ask for more?"

On Tuesday, March 3, the Dodgers hosted the Hillmen of Platteville in the first game of the state tournament in the Dodgeville Sub-Regional. The atmosphere was electric. The sellout crowd poured in. Marking the first quarter were a series of miscues by both squads. The play became frenzied and physical and the resulting whistles brought incensed fans to their feet. A high-scoring first quarter allowed the Dodgers a slim 2 point lead, at 20-18. In the second quarter, Dodgeville

a score of 77-72. In a celebratory mood, the Dodger team gathered at point guard Bruce Harrison's home following the game. The players were proud of their accomplishment but they understood there was much more work to do. It was now on to the Sub-Sectional for the Dodgers.

Bloomington was next up for the Dodgers as they traveled to the Lancaster Sub-Sectional on March 10th. The winner of this contest would go to the Sectional. As the game began, the Dodger's height advantage became obvious. Vogt, the Blue Jays' center, scored the first points of the game, but a Bob Rock field goal and a 3-point play by Corky Evans gave Dodgeville a 5-2 lead. The Dodgers' outside shots were not falling, but they pounded the offensive boards successfully. In addition to put-backs, several fast-break baskets allowed Dodgeville to cruise to a 23-6 first-quarter lead and to push the lead to 44-22 at the intermission. The second half was more of the same. The Dodgers scored another 44 points while holding the Blue Jays to only 24. The final score was Dodgeville 88 and Bloomington 46. Pat Flynn led Dodgeville with 26 points. Rick Brown scored 22. Johnson led the Blue Jays with 10 points.

The teams were now finalized for the Platteville Sectional to begin play on Friday, March 13th. Monroe would play Belmont in game one and Dodgeville would take on Soldiers Grove in the second. The first game was no contest as the Monroe Cheesemakers put together a solid effort and easily defeated Belmont 81-47. The nightcap would see Dodgeville tipping it off with the Cardinals of Soldiers Grove. The winner would play Monroe for the Sectional final with a chance to go to Madison as a member of the elite eight.

With their aggressive play from the get-go, the Dodgers came out with vengeance, taking a first quarter lead of 24-13. With a lock-down defense and a fast-break style they overwhelmed the undermanned Cardinals. The half-time score was 45-20, Dodgers. The second half provided much of the same, even when the Dodgers subbed for their starters. The running style employed by Dodgeville worked well, and was in sharp contrast to the far more deliberate style of a year ago. The final score was 85-42, Dodgeville. It had all started on the boards where the Dodgers had outrebounded Soldiers Grove by a 44 to 23 margin. Offensively, the Dodgers clicked on 38 of 83 shots while the Cardinals made only 12 of 48. Ten Dodgers made their way into the scoring column. The Dodgers were led by Pat Flynn with 19, Bob Rock with 15 and Rick Brown and Dick Stephens with 10 points and 9 points respectively. For the Cardinals, Dull scored 9 points. The next opponent for the Dodgers would be one of their biggest rivals, Monroe. The Cheesemakers felt they were ready for the challenge and had vowed to make Swiss cheese out of the Dodger defense.

It was all on the line as Dodgeville and Monroe played for the sectional title. The winner would go to Madison. Barely one short year ago, these same two teams had battled for the sectional trophy in what had proved to be a fierce contest. Dodgeville had prevailed in that contest by a score of 64-50. The Cheesemakers were determined to avenge the defeat.

Coming off a convincing sectional semi-final victory over Belmont, 81-47, Monroe was confident, primed and ready to go. Their team featured some talented juniors who would go on to play basketball at the next level—Keith Burington (UW-Madison), Bob Buchholtz (UW-Whitewater), and Tom Mitchell (UW-Madison).

The contest was tight from the beginning. The Dodgers began the game error prone as they turned the ball over six times in the first quarter. Fortunately, their superb defense limited Monroe from getting any good looks. Bob Rock put the defensive clamps on shooting sensation guard Tom Mitchell, son of Monroe coach Lee Mitchell. Dodgeville Coach Wilson knew his team could not run with the high-scoring Cheesemakers so he decided to take the air out of the ball. The game seesawed and was tied eight times in the first half leaving the score at the intermission 24-24. In the third period Bob Rock's three shots broke the game wide open. Dodgeville then continued to control the tempo and maintained its advantage in the rebounding department. The Dodgers cruised to a 59-48 victory and once again the sectional championship and a trip to Madison was theirs. For the evening, Rick Brown had 22 points and 13 rebounds. Bob Rock scored 17 points and had 10 rebounds while Pat Flynn added 12 points and 8 rebounds. For Monroe, Burington was high with 15 points, then Dearth with 12 and Buchholtz with 10. Guard Tom Mitchell was held to 2 points. Lee Mitchell, Monroe's coach, felt that he had underestimated the Dodgers and their ability to control the game once they had a lead.

"Once they get ahead of you, they kill you," he put it. For Monroe, this would mark their fifth loss in their last six sectional final games. Wilson, ecstatic, commended his team on their defensive effort, "These kids are really proud of their defense, more so than their ability to score. We styled it after Cincinnati and plant ourselves on the baselines." For the second year in a row, the Dodgers would represent their sectional in Madison. And, for the second year in a row they had eliminated Monroe, their biggest rival, in the process.

Recently I caught up with 1964 Monroe star Keith Burington, who went on to an equally stellar career at UW-Madison. I asked him about the difficulty the Cheesemakers had against the Dodgers. "When Dodgeville slowed the game down in 1963, it was a complete surprise," he told me. "They had been fast-breaking and scoring big all year and we weren't prepared. However, when we met in 1964, we had a hunch they would employ their ball-control tactic again. That we started out cold didn't help matters. They continued to secure the paint with their big bodies. It was so crowded in the lane, in fact, that a guy needed a shoehorn to secure a rebound. And once they got the lead, it was very difficult to catch up. You have to credit Wilson and Dodgeville. They were able to run the floor when needed but, at a moment's notice, turn off the switch with ball control. Amazing coaching!"

Burington's teammate Bob Buchholtz, who went on to play at UW-Whitewater and later became an administrator in the Waukesha School District, compared the two teams.

"Like us," Bob said, "Dodgeville had an experienced coach, seasoned players, great teamwork, and great balance. Being a small school, they grew together much as we did. However, they were bigger and senior-laden. The Dodgers changing the tempo with their methodical style and their deciding not to run had a significant effect on the game and its outcome."

The ride home was very exciting as the Dodgers passed through the neighboring cities from Platteville to Dodgeville. Mineral Point and other friendly foes escorted the Dodgers through their cities with their police cars and fire trucks. If that wasn't enough, they were greeted by huge crowds lining the streets back in Dodgeville. Here too, police cars and fire trucks were out.

By night's end it was official. The final eight teams to make their way to Madison for the tournament would be Waterloo, Waukesha, Milwaukee North, Merrill, Manitowoc, Eau Claire Memorial, Frederic, and Dodgeville. On Tuesday, March 17, the *Milwaukee Sentinel* featured an article regarding the coaches' tournament favorite. North was the unanimous choice. "We have the confidence to go all the way," said North coach Vic Anderson. "North has to be favored. Dodgeville and Eau Claire will be tough. We've got our work cut out for us," said Jim Dietrick, coach of defending champion Manitowoc. Eau Claire Memorial coach Harry Gibbs and Merrill coach Jerry Eckman hedged a bit on the North prediction, making Dodgeville, the meets only unbeaten entry, the co-favorite. "They both got tournament experience going for them," said Eckman. Eckman's team would be meeting Dodgeville in the tournament opener. Lastly, Coach John Wilson not counting his own team out by any means, still voted for North. "They play a lot of basketball in Milwaukee. They have a real good playground program. I'd have to pick North," he said.

The Dodgers would not play until Thursday's first game at state, against Merrill at 1:30 p.m. The Monroe game had been very physical, and the five days remaining before the next game would give the Dodgers time to heal and lick their wounds. However, their roster would need to be trimmed for them to meet the WIAA ruling that allowed each team to only carry 12 players for tournament play in Madison. This meant that six people would not get the opportunity to participate at state. Now with a good practice on Monday and an even better one on Tuesday, the Dodgers felt they were more than ready. Their next practice was scheduled for Wednesday at 1:30 p.m. in the UW Fieldhouse.

The Dodgers were confident as they exited the Dodgeville gym on Tuesday. Rick Brown said, "The team should get the record, we're going all the way at state this time." Bruce Harrison stated, "This is something to remember as a senior, going to state, and we can't wait to get there. I've been looking forward to it all year. We're 23-0 and that counts." Finally Curt Anderson added this, "This will be my first time at state. I consider it quite a privilege to go up there. The team is ready."

The year had gone by quickly. It seemed like only yesterday that the Dodgers were being welcomed home by a city gone wild after their stellar performance. They had exceeded everyone's expectations with last year's second-place finish. For tiny Dodgeville, a return trip seemed much like a fairy tale to many. Yet here they were, poised and ready once again to represent the people of Dodgeville, a close-knit city devoted to its beloved Dodgers as much as its Dodgers were devoted to them.

Wednesday brought a 9:00 a.m. pep rally in the school gymnasium. At 9:30 the team was honored with a massive send-off by their fans. Mayor of Dodgeville, J. Clifford Olson, addressed the assembly and wished the team good luck. The Chamber of Commerce and the Kiwanis Club were present. The school band, cheerleaders, and the town's fire trucks were on hand to add to the spectacle. The atmosphere was reminiscent of the scene of their return from one year ago. Many of the players were interviewed as to their thoughts about the upcoming state tournament. Win or lose, the players would not return back home until after Saturday night's final game. Since Monday, businesses in Dodgeville had been starting to close for the week. It was becoming very difficult for any student to concentrate on academics any longer.

As the two Dodger team vans made their way up highway 18-151 towards Madison, they were escorted by a caravan of cars. When the players looked back at the line of cars in formation, they could literally observe how their fans were behind them and feel a distinct sense of pride, of mission. As the team continued its journey through the neighboring communities, written signs of support were displayed by each small town.

Upon their arrival in Madison, and after settling into their dorm rooms, the players were in for a treat as player Kramer Rock explains: "We played our first game on Thursday. Wednesday night we were taken to the Orpheum Theater on the Square in Madison. The movie was *Cleopatra*, with Elizabeth Taylor. Odd as this is, there was a lot of rib-elbowing and snickering, as Ms. Taylor revealed body parts on a 50' screen most of us only dreamed about. I still remember this event."

Tomorrow would be a day of great importance. The Dodgers needed to be prepared and ready for their first-round matchup with Merrill, the first game of the day. For now, it was time to get some rest and dream of the important thoughts on their minds. After that movie, there may have been several!

Again thousands of fans had converged on Madison. The atmosphere was electric! As per custom, the players were housed in the campus dorms, a convenient location. Dodgeville stayed at Humphrey Hall, just north of the UW Fieldhouse by about four blocks, right on Lake Mendota. They dined at the Terrace Cafeteria, only two blocks from Humphrey Hall. The dorm site allowed for an easy walk to the Field House for practice and games.

With the protocol basically the same as the previous year, Day One of the tournament would feature four games, two in the afternoon and two at night. The first game on the docket for this day would feature Dodgeville taking on Merrill. With the sun glaring through the large Field House windows during the afternoon games, the earlier contests did not appear to have the same ambiance as the night games. Nevertheless, each team's fan base soon made that factor irrelevant, erupting into prolonged applause as its honored team took the floor. Again the distinct echoing of the loud Field House horn soon brought back memories of a year before.

On Thursday, March 19, 1964, the first game was ready to begin. As the game commenced both teams came out in zone defenses. Dodgeville scored three early baskets, but then fell into a four-plus-minute drought. Merrill, equally as skittish, scored only one basket in nearly the first five minutes of the game. The Dodgers held a slim 8-6 lead at the quarter. Neither team could crack the other's defense. Both teams were turning the ball over. The game seesawed back and forth with neither team taking command. Merrill took a slight 3-point lead going into half-time at 18-15. Then, in what would be one of the closest games of the tournament, Dodgeville tied the score at 31 all, before again trailing by two. Finally the Dodgers came to life. Pat Flynn scored off an offensive rebound, Rick Brown hit a short jumper and Flynn added two more from the charity stripe to give the Dodgers a hopeful four-point lead with barely two minutes remaining. Koski of Merrill answered back on a short shot, but Dodgeville's Rick Brown and Bruce Harrison each added a score giving the Dodgers a 6-point lead with a minute and a half left in the contest. Merrill didn't quit as Tom Fox scored two and Jim Langenkamp added 2 free throws making the score 45-43 Dodgeville with only three seconds remaining. Two free throws by Harrison and one by Brown sealed the victory giving the Dodgers a 48-43 win. In the end, Dodgeville shot 39 percent from the floor on 18 of 46 attempts, while Merrill with nine more shots was 18 for 55 shooting 33 percent. Flynn led Dodgeville with 14 points while Brown added 12. Wilson, well aware his team did not play well, offered an assessment, "We won and I guess that's the main thing. But we turned the ball over to them too many times. One thing I am happy about is our defense." In a twist of fate: Merrill star Jim Langenkamp had been born in Dodgeville!

In the second afternoon game, a big and tough Eau Claire Memorial team took on Waukesha. Playing against a much taller team, Waukesha traded baskets with the Old Abes for most of the first half. They utilized full-court pressure against their taller opponent. The inside presence of 6'9" Loehnis and 6'7" Ellenson for Eau Claire was equalized by the incredible shooting display from Waukesha's Mike Grainger, who scored 22 points in the first half. The game was extremely tight with the score knotted at 39 all at half-time. The game remained close until late in the third quarter when the Blackshirts inserted reserve Ted Bear. Known more as the star running back on Waukesha's undefeated Milwaukee Suburban Conference Champion football team, Bear turned the game around immediately with his adept ball-handling, pinpoint passing, and timely scoring. Waukesha ran off 10 straight as Bear found his teammates with great passes, and secured a 6-point lead for the Blackshirts at the end of the third quarter. Eau Claire was never able to overcome this run, but did cut a nine-point deficit to four pints with twenty seconds left. Here again Bear—celebrating his eighteenth birthday—answered with two free throws sealing the win and giving Waukesha a 78-71 victory. For the evening Grainger led Waukesha with 32 points on 14 of 26 attempts. The Blackshirts outrebounded the Old Abes by a margin of 55-45. Tom Hansis led Eau Claire with 27.

The first evening saw Frederic meet Waterloo. The game which would end up extremely close had large momentum swings for each team. Frederic took an 8-point lead by the end of the first quarter with several baskets by 6'6" Joe McAbee, who was able to get free underneath the basket. He scored 9 points in the first quarter. The half saw the score knotted at 29 all, thanks to a scoring spree by Waterloo's Battist, Reige and Gorder. However, again in the third period, Frederic's Joe McAbee took control with several key baskets, allowing his team to take a two-point lead going into the final period. With just over three minutes to go, Waterloo was down four points before Dave Battist hit two shots in a row to tie the score at 56-56. With under a minute left, Frederic was called for traveling. Waterloo quickly took a timeout. Waterloo then played for last shot and eventually found Rhode under the basket with 15 seconds remaining to take a 58-56 lead. A last-second shot by Frederic's Brad McAbee rolled off the rim, giving Waterloo the two-point victory. Waterloo's Battist scored 25 points and hauled in 11 boards. Reige scored 17 points and Rhode contributed 10 rebounds besides the winning basket. For Frederic, Joe McAbee scored 22 points and had 12 rebounds and Jack Orgeman added 14 points.

In the final game of the evening, the reigning state champion, Manitowoc would take on favored Milwaukee North. Blanton Simmons of North wasted no time, hitting a long-range jumper to start the game. This was countered by Manitowoc's Bob Sullivan, who made three of four shots from the field, allowing the Ships to score eight straight points against North's zone press. North quickly shifted into a man-to-man press. Manitowoc's Sullivan subsequently picked up three fouls in the first quarter and sat out for five minutes in the second period. North, which trailed by two points at the end of the first quarter, responded offensively.

Star guard Simmons continued his hot streak, making 9 of 15 shots from the floor to give the Blue Devils a 35-28 cushion at the half. Early in the third period, North's Simmons limped off the floor, having tweaked his knee. Now it was Esthesial Ford's time to take over offensively for North. From that point on, Ford scored 19 points keeping North's lead intact. The end of the third quarter found North up by eight points. Sullivan, who played little in the third quarter, fouled out in the fourth. Without him the Ships could never regain control. The final score was North 76 and Manitowoc 63.

Besides his torrid shooting in the second half, Ford pulled down 21 of North's 66 rebounds for the night. He finished with 24 points for the evening, matching the scoring of his teammate Simmons. Manitowoc, playing without Sullivan much of the night, was led by Dave Jansson, who scored 24.

With Day One complete, four teams were left in contention for the state title. Milwaukee North, Waukesha, Waterloo and Dodgeville had made it through day one unscathed and each still believed they could win the title.

The first consolation game on Friday, March 20 would feature Merrill and Eau Claire Memorial. The losers of the afternoon games would no longer be in the tournament. A very close game saw Eau Claire take a three-point lead into the quarter only to have Merrill come back and tie the game at half, 30-30. Late in the third quarter Merrill turned the tie game into a 50-46 lead, widening the gap to 54-46 early in the fourth. It was at this point the game quickly changed. Several turnovers and inaccurate shooting gave the taller

Old Abes an opportunity to get back in the game. With less than six minutes remaining, the game was again tied, 54-54. Eau Claire's Bert Smith had come up with four timely points to lead the surge. Then once again it was Smith, whose long-range shot gave Eau Claire a 56-54 lead. With over three minutes left, the lead was 60-55 Eau Claire. With two and one-half minutes left and the score 60-57, Merrill's Langenkamp fouled out, severely hurting Merrill's chances. However, Merrill cut the lead to 62-61 and had possession of the ball with 6 seconds remaining. But the intended play backfired, allowing Eau Claire to add a free throw and walk away with the victory by a score of 63-61. Mike Loehnis, Eau Claire's 6'9" center, paced his team with 22 points while Tom Hansis added 15. For Merrill, Jim Kioski scored 16 points and Langenkamp added 14. The Old Abes would now be in Saturday's consolation championship game.

The second consolation game pitted Frederic against Manitowoc. The Ships took an early lead with a short jumper by Bob Sullivan who scored four baskets in the first quarter. It was over six minutes before Frederic scored its first basket, making the score 9-2. Manitowoc, who held a 25-20 lead at half, increased the lead to 10 points on several occasions, only to have a surging Frederic, led by 6'6" Joe McAbee, come back to within a point, 28-27, with four minutes left in the third quarter. With less than four minutes to go in the final period, the Ships held a 3-point lead. Suddenly the Vikings' shooting went cold to leave them outscored by a 10-2 margin as Manitowoc took control the rest of the way and coasted to

on 21 of 48 attempts while Waukesha hit 14 for 54 for 26 percent. Incredibly, up to this point the lowest offensive production by the Blackshirts this year had been 68 points against Milwaukee Suburban Conference foe Shorewood. Once again Dodgeville had derailed a speeding train by controlling the tempo.

Not too long ago, I caught up with Mike Grainger and asked about the game. He remembered the night well. "Dodgeville controlled the tempo and was very physical with our big guys," he told me. "I hadn't seen Dodgeville play or even knew where the city was located in Wisconsin. Part of our game Dodgeville utilized a 'box and one' defense with the one player guarding me and the rest zoning. We did not adjust to this very well. You have to give the Dodgers credit for their effort. They deserved the game."

I recently had the opportunity to speak with Charlie Miller, Waukesha's coach, who remembered his encounter with the Dodgers well. Having successfully pressed the lanky Eau Claire team in the quarter-final, he thought Dodgeville might be susceptible as well. But he told me, "The Dodgers were extremely well-coached and had no problem with our full-court pressure. They shut down Grainger and controlled the tempo of the game." Exiting the court after the Dodgeville game, Miller ran into North Coach Victor Anderson. "So how do you think we would match up with Dodgeville?" Anderson asked him. Miller recalls how he thought for a second, then replied, "Your full-court press would destroy them!"

The evening's second semi-final game featured Waterloo and Milwaukee North. Predicted to be a high-scoring event, it lived up to its billing. Waterloo opened the game quickly taking a 13-6 lead with easy shots around the basket due to North's defensive lapses. North quickly adjusted, controlling the boards and evening the score at 19-19. It was at this point that North's star guard, Blanton Simmons, took over. Simmons scored three quick baskets to give North a 25-19 lead at the end of the first period. Incredibly, he made 10 of 14 shots in the second quarter alone to give the Blue Devils a commanding 51-37 half-time lead. As a team, North made 13 of 23 attempts in the period. With over 50 points at half, North's fans were yelling for the Blue Devils to reach the 100-point mark.

In the third period Waterloo refused to die and staged a comeback. A North cold spell allowed the Pirates to cut the lead to only five late in the third quarter. A long jump shot by Simmons gave the Blue Devils a 65-58 advantage at the end of three periods. Determined to break the game open, North outscored Waterloo 12-6 to open the final quarter. With a comfortable 13-point lead in hand, Simmons fouled out with approximately five minutes left in the contest. At that point, both teams traded baskets for the rest of the game. The final score was North 94 and Waterloo 81. North's 94 points exceeded by one point the tournament record set in 1962 by Milwaukee Lincoln against Eau Claire. It had been an entertaining game. Blanton Simmons had a huge night with 36 points on 17 of 25 shooting. Esthesial Ford added 21 points and 19 rebounds. Gene Riege led the Pirates with 29 points while Dave Battist chipped in 27.

The stage was now set for the next day's state-championship game. Milwaukee North versus Dodgeville. "Shooting vs. Defense in Final" was the headline of the Milwaukee Journal on March 21. Two contrasting styles would be on the line come tomorrow. When asked about the match-up with North in the final, Dodgeville's Wilson was adamant, "We need to slow them down. We've got to try anyhow." As for Dodgeville's offense and their smothering zone defense, North's Anderson remarked, "I don't know what we can do with them. They shot 49 percent for the season and we shot 47 percent. And their defense is tremendous. It looks as though they shoot better than we do and defend better." Yes, Saturday night would prove to be an interesting night of basketball and both teams seemed more than prepared for the challenge.

Chapter Eight

On Saturday March 21, 1964, the final day of the Wisconsin Boys State Basketball Tournament was finally here. It certainly felt much cozier in the gym than the brisk 20-degree temperature and standing inch of snow outside. What had started in early November of 1963—the dreams of summer put into hard, earnest effort—was now at its March, 1964 conclusion. By the end of this day, we would be crowning a new Wisconsin State High School Basketball Champion for 1964.

The first game of the day featured the Eau Claire Memorial Old Abes playing Manitowoc for the consolation championship. Playing for the consolation championship, Manitowoc and Eau Claire would be meeting for the fourth time in tournament play. A very close game in the first quarter, Eau Claire took the lead several times, only to have Manitowoc fight back for an 18-16 lead at the quarter. In quarter two the Ships' Sullivan took over scoring 12 of his team's 25 points to give his team an insurmountable 43-26 lead at half. The Old Abes fought back and cut the deficit to ten at 50-40, but Manitowoc staged another rally and the margin went to 17 points again, 63-46, by the end of the third quarter. But Manitowoc was not done. They scored 28 points in the final period to win the game by a margin of 91-65. Manitowoc's Sullivan, only a junior, scored a game-high 24 points while Dave Jansson scored 17 and Bill Buerstatte added 13. Eau Claire's Tom Hansis led the Old Abes with 16 points. For the evening Manitowoc shot 53 percent from the floor while Eau Claire was at a 34 percent clip. For the Ships, it was their third consolation championship in the last seven years and they finished the season with an 18-7 record. The old Abes finished their campaign 23-3.

The next game of the evening, the third-place game, featured the Blackshirts of Waukesha and the Waterloo Pirates. Waukesha jumped on Waterloo right from the start, building a nine-point lead in the first two minutes. However, the Pirates were not about to concede the game and rallied back trailing 24-23 at the end of the first quarter, thanks to 10 points from Gene Reige. Then with Reige in foul trouble, the Blackshirts blew the game wide open and led by a 50-38 margin at half. Waukesha had made 22 of 39 shot attempts in the first half, led by Dick Martin with 18. The Blackshirts stretched the lead to 18 in the third quarter before Waterloo again staged another rally. Twice the Pirates closed to within three before Waukesha finally put them away by a score of 99-76. The 99 points shattered the single game record of 94 set by Milwaukee North only the day before. With Reige sitting out most of the game, Dave Battist led the Pirates with 21 points and Dick Gorder contributed 16. For Waukesha five players were in double figures led by Dick Martin with 29 and Mike Grainger with 16. The third place win was the 17th of the season for Waukesha, against nine losses. Waterloo ended the season with a very respectable 23-4 record and a fourth-place finish in the tournament.

Next on the docket was the grand finale, the state championship final. Two tremendous teams with remarkable seasons under their belts were now set to be matched.

Milwaukee North, 24-1, had an outstanding cast of stars, some of whose next stops would be at the major-college level. Their only season blemish had been to a very talented Rufus King team by a score of 61-50. Dodgeville, 25-0, had clawed its way to the final with a balanced blue-collar, team approach.

Both schools were well represented by their fans. Several Dodgeville busses and a long line of cars seemed to have brought every resident of Dodgeville to Madison. It seemed that everyone and his cousin had an emotional interest in this game. The Dodgeville band was on hand in full force. The team's cheerleaders, who had been in Madison since Wednesday, each had their hair done bouffant-style at a local beauty shop in honor of the special occasion. Decked out in their spanking-new, black wool sweaters featuring a Dodger team button, they had opted not to wear the traditional white sweaters with a black D, edged in orange.

Coming into the contest the Dodger team had to feel confident and good about themselves after their semi-final thrashing of Waukesha. Dodgeville had joined a select group by getting to the final game. They were one of eight teams ever to have made it to the championship game two years in a row. Coincidentally, Milwaukee North was in that group— and just as convinced of its invincibility, having put up 94 in its defeat of Waterloo.

To win a state championship *everything* must fall into place. Every detail and element must be addressed and accounted for. It can come down to what you eat, how you sleep or even how much your mind is on the game. A team must start strongly, confident, and master the emotional highs and lows that constantly present themselves. A coach and players must make good game decisions and adeptly adjust to counter the instantaneous ebbs and flows that can occur at a moment's notice. Do you stay with the game plan or do you alter it? The team must be on the same page and everyone must work for the betterment of the 'team.' How the referees are calling the game is extremely important and must be a consideration. Today's championship game would be called by two outstanding WIAA officials, Duaine Counsell and Gale Zimmerman. A bit of luck is always nice and can oftentimes conceal one's flaws. It certainly doesn't hurt to have a positive, hard-nose attitude, often construed as cockiness by your opponents. Additionally, a team must believe that a state championship is its birthright or legacy. Finally, a coach must build mutual trust with his players to insure they perform as a cohesive unit. Each of the coaches in this final game was a veteran with a lengthy and impressive track record and unique approaches to the game. There were thousands of fans on hand and many, many thousands more gazing at their screens—all anticipating a showcasing of two distinct and contrasting philosophies. Moreover, one team was from a populated, inner-city school and the other was a small-town, country squad. Which one would prevail would soon be evident.

Ned Moton, a reserve guard for Milwaukee North in 1964, recalls the Blue Devil team chalk talk in the dorms,

the bottom defender in the 1-3-1. His sheer hustle allowed the Dodgers to cover both corners, where the 1-3-1 was most susceptible. His teammates' defensive slides and constant help made his job all the easier. As a team they talked on defense, alerting each other to breakdowns and pitfalls as North continued its assault.

North had placed Simmons at the top of the key. Here, Bruce Harrison was stationed and applied great pressure to the North player. Harrison describes, "Coach Wilson had given me a directive, 'Don't let Blanton Simmons' right leg go past your left knee,' he had insisted, 'and if you do, you'll be sitting on the bench next to me.'" Wilson felt that Simmons was much more vulnerable when forced to his left or weak hand. The hunch seemed to be paying off, as Simmons had not yet hit a field goal in the first quarter. When North utilized the one-guard alignment with Simmons at the top of the zone, Dodgeville continued with its standard 1-3-1 with man-to-man principles. If the Blue Devils answered with a two-guard front, which they did only on a few occasions, the Dodgers quickly inverted their defensive alignment to a 2-1-2 match-up zone, still utilizing "closest man theory." This sleight-of-hand shift made it difficult for the Blue Devils to properly align themselves offensively and kept them off balance all evening. The tactical change of a flexing defense by Wilson was disguised beautifully, implemented perfectly. Wilson called this alignment his "Diamond Zone," because the Dodgers could easily change their defensive positioning from a princess (square) cut to a marquise (diamond) cut. The Dodgeville defense could best be compared to a chameleon, changing its colors at the first sign of danger. Another enormous benefit was the fact that Dodgeville could make these adjustments without having to waste precious timeouts.

Dodgeville, however, did not shine on offense. They were unable to get the ball inside to their premier post player, Rick Brown. Additionally, they were unable to connect on several free throw attempts. In a logical move to up-tempo the game, North began to harass the Dodgers with both a full-court zone and man-to-man press. In addition, they used a two-man trap in the half-court. Regardless, neither team seemed to be playing up to their capabilities. As a result, North never built the commanding lead they had anticipated and settled on a low scoring 12-9 lead at the end of the first quarter.

The second quarter started much the same, with the two teams sparring back and forth. At one point with North up by five, North lost the ball on four straight possessions without even a shot attempt. The Blue Devils seemed to be hurrying the game and playing too fast. This in turn caused them to travel, miss easy layups and throw errant passes. At this same time the Dodgers stayed patient, breaking the full-court and half-court pressure applied by North, but they still could not score with ease. The Dodgers continued to make at least five passes with each possession, being careful not to throw any cross-court passes against their quick opponents. Wilson had told his team to make sure they stayed within the framework of their offense and that 'freelancing' would not be allowed tonight. As 1964 junior player Kramer Rock put it, "Freelancing was like cussing in church."

Near the end of the first half, Dodger Corky Evans and North's Esthesiel Ford were involved in what appeared to be an obvious jump ball. With neither player about to relinquish possession, they both struggled for the upper hand. The six-foot Evans eventually pulled the huge center over his shoulder like a bale of hay back on the farm in Dodgeville and Ford came crashing to the floor amid a sea of "oohs and ahs." As 1962-63 Dodgeville assistant coach John Crubaugh recounted, "I thought wow, what an important happening in this game. Dodgeville isn't going to back down to the big-city boys."

With both teams continuing to play subpar ball, North coasted into half-time with a 23-19 lead. For the half, North had made only 11 of 42 shot attempts while Dodgeville was slightly better with 9 of 24.

In the locker room, Wilson insisted that the Dodgers stick to his game plan. He knew that if they did, they could prevail. Dodgeville player Dick Stephens related, "Weenie came in and said something like, 'We can beat these guys!!' But he said it in such a way that we knew we could just beat them. I am not so sure anyone thought we could, but when he said that I felt he planted a 'state championship' attitude in our heads."

Meanwhile, North's Coach Anderson was deeply concerned. His team's pressure had not altered the tempo of the game. His team did not seem to be playing up to its capabilities. He encouraged the Blue Devils to do so. Attempting to reinforce their confidence, he told his team there were two halves to every game and the second would be theirs.

As the third quarter began, the game continued to seesaw back and forth much like the first half. With North in a full-court press, Dodgeville's Bob Rock was bringing the ball up the floor against a very quick North guard. In a moment of desperation, Rock dribbled the ball between a Blue Devil defender's legs and retrieved it on the other side. The crowd went berserk. This flamboyant play might have been expected by North, but none-the-less was made by a conservative Dodgeville player. With under six minutes left in the third quarter, North now clung to a two-point lead.

The next four minutes would prove to be the evening's most significant. It was during this critical span that Dodgeville scored 12 straight unanswered points. The combination of a free throw by Harrison, three field goals and a free throw by Brown, and scores by Evans and Rock gave the Dodgers a formidable 35-25 lead with two minutes left in the quarter. Dodgeville further frustrated the Blue Devils with ball control and tough defense taking a lead of 36-29 going into the final quarter. The third quarter had proved to be instrumental for the Dodgers as they made 7 of 11 attempts from the floor. Dodgeville had outscored North 17-6 in the quarter.

With only one quarter to go, North was still struggling to turn the tide. Dodgeville continued to command the tempo and the hurried pace of the Blue Devils caused more miscues and frustration. With great patience, Dodgeville continued their deliberate four-corner offense, making sure to be strong with the basketball and to make the additional pass. North continued to pester the Dodgers with a variety of pressures but, as a result, fouled much too often. It soon became a game of cat and mouse resulting in the Dodgers going to the foul line 21 times in the final period and calmly sinking 19 foul shots. This statistic alone, the direct result of Dodgeville's patience, was far too much for the North squad to overcome. As the quarter dwindled away, the crowd seemingly sensed an improbable Dodger victory was now becoming a distinct reality. Dodgeville scored only two field goals in the last quarter but, with the addition of 19 free throws, outscored the Blue Devils by a margin of 23-16. The 1964 state championship belonged to Dodgeville by a score of 59-45.

For the evening Dodgeville shot 47 percent from the floor making 18 of 38 attempts. North shot a miserable 26 percent making only 19 of 71 shots. Dodgeville's Rick Brown may have lost the center tip at the beginning of the game, but as the game progressed he was out-jumping everyone. Brown led the Dodgers with 20 points and 9 rebounds. Bob Rock scored 14 points while Corky Evans scored 12 points and pulled down 11 boards. For North, Esthesial Ford scored 17 points and had 11 rebounds. Tom Martin had 14 points while Clarence Young added 13 rebounds. Blanton Simmons was held to 3 points on a very cool 1 of 16 from the floor.

Incredibly, despite all of North's pressure, the Dodgers committed only four turnovers in the game.

When asked to tell the press what was going through his mind at half-time, Coach Wilson replied, "I knew then that we would win." He continued, "I wasn't really sure before the game but I knew at half. North had tried to make us play their game but we didn't play it. Our boys stuck to their instructions. That's what I mean about discipline."

Star guard Bob Buchholtz, whose Monroe team the Dodgers had eliminated in the sectional final, attended the title game. "Watching the Dodgeville-Milwaukee North game was almost a déjà vu experience," he recalls. "Controlling the tempo and slowing down North was precisely what the Dodgers had done to us."

I asked Bob Rock if he remembered about being under pressure and drilling through the legs of the North player in the third quarter. He did remember and acknowledged, "I never looked for opportunities to do stuff like that. It wasn't a grandstanding effort, it was the only option, and in a split second after it, I remember thinking about being pulled by Coach and in my next dribble thinking how that must have angered the North player and that I would eventually pay for it." He then assessed North's pressure in the final period. "I just remember wanting to get the ball over the half-court line by pass or dribble. I don't remember consciously thinking about that job, but I remember running like a rabbit being shot at. I remember throwing a couple welcomed long passes to a wide-open Rick Brown under the basket towards the end

Hysteria, pandemonium, disbelief and awe describe the reaction of the players and their fans as the clock ticked closer and closer to the final seconds. The game's last few minutes had people from both teams literally crying with emotion as the Dodgers edged closer to victory and the Blue Devils fell. Fans were jumping up and down, hugging, kissing. Screams of excitement filled the air. North's Blue Devil players had given their all until the end, but the determined Dodgers had continued their relentless push to victory. With the final sound of the Field House horn, the crowd and viewers all across the state came to realize what they had seen—perhaps the greatest game in the facility's history.

The trophy presentation came before the cheering and adoring crowd. Coach Anderson and the Blue Devils received their award first and demonstrated great dignity in accepting the second-place trophy. Now it was Dodgeville's turn. The roaring crowd came to its feet and showed its appreciation for the Dodgers and their accomplishment. Wilson and his group of mighty mites lifted the trophy proudly and the Field House erupted all the more. The team posed for pictures, and the celebration was on. Wilson would not let his team cut down the nets via tradition. Formally receiving the trophy was more than enough, he felt. He did, however, send a man to collect one of the nets after the arena had cleared.

A Who's Who of high school players and coaches were in attendance. George Faherty was a junior member of the Platteville team, conference (SWAL) rivals of Dodgeville who lost to the Dodgers in the first regional game. George recounted his effort to congratulate them for the big win. "We got to know the Dodgeville kids pretty well. I can remember being on the edge of the court when they won the state title and congratulating them," he tells me. "My high school coach, Royce Reeves, who is from Dodgeville, got upset. He came running down out of the stands and said, 'What the heck are you guys doing?!' That's how it was in those days. You didn't make friends with opposing players. He didn't want us congratulating them."

Arriving in Madison, it had been a gutsy call by Wilson to alter his team's bread and butter, the man-to-man defense, in favor of the 1-3-1 match-up. It was reported that Wilson further tweaked his defense the morning of the championship game in a team walk-through. Leaders lead and do not shy away from decisions that require courage. But his new defensive philosophy had more than altered his defensive alignment. It was an ideal modification for his team as it had perfectly complemented his overall defensive concept but still utilized the man-to-man principles he so relished. The defense's ever changing chameleon aspect had caused great havoc. In addition, it gave the team the best chance to exploit its defensive intelligence and to provide each player with additional help against a very talented opponent. But more than anything, it greatly confused the North team and took them out of its rhythm.

Beyond the new innovative defense, the Dodgers still had exercised their deliberate offense. This part of their philosophy might have been subject to change had North gotten off to a better start. Had the Blue Devils taken that commanding lead, it may have been an entirely different story. As it turned out, Dodgeville had never been in a rigorous catch-up mode. The Dodger defense had limited North's good looks. North's effort to up-tempo the game, in an effort to make up for its cold shooting, had only brought more frustration. North had to expend great effort on defense in their attempt to get the ball back. Many times this had led to hurried miscues on offense leaving them once again playing half-court defense against a patient, well-oiled machine. Sometimes these long defensive spells had lasted more than twelve passes. The key for Dodgeville had been to keep their cool, to get a lead, and out-patience the opponent. Coach Wilson had predicted correctly: His 'team' *would* win the state tournament. With Wilson at the helm, his team played outstanding and to the level of expertise he had anticipated they could. Very simply, the Dodgeville team followed Coach Wilson's plan to a T, allowing them to perform at a much greater level than the sum of their parts.

Dodgeville's Corky Evans explained, "We won because of Coach Wilson. We had a super game plan for North, plus we followed it. There is no doubt that Coach Wilson was the number-one factor in winning. We played as a complete team. No one cared about their stats. A second factor in winning was that we all had played in the championship game the previous year, 1963, against a very good Manitowoc team." Corky continued, "Against North, we played the best half of basketball that we've ever played together."

Other players offered their takes. Curt Anderson simply summed it up this way: "Milwaukee North did not think that they could lose." Teammate Tom Schleck added, "Wilson had scouted Milwaukee North and had a great game plan. He identified where each of North's players liked to take their shots from and made sure a Dodgeville player got to the spot first, which frustrated the Milwaukee North player." I asked teammate Mike Collins what made the Dodgers click and eventually gain the victory? He replied, "We clicked because all the practice both during and off-season made us better. We clicked because of the confidence we had in each other. We all participated in our winning ways since grade school. We won because we believed we could and should because we worked hard and listened to our coaches." Point guard Bruce Harrison added this, "Our team never had one person act like they thought they were better than the other. We five (Bob, Corky, Rick, Pat and I) were very close. We played together since 7th grade. We were cousins, neighbors, and Jinx (Pat Flynn) was my best friend. I loved him. He was loyal and easy-going."

Center Rick Brown knew exactly why his team won. "Our coaching was outstanding and our teamwork superb. But very simply, we knew each other so well. Going back to grade school, some of us public school kids would go over to St. Joe's and practice with the Catholic team twice each week. Even at this early age our group of guys was starting to bond." I asked player Dick Stephens what factors helped

Dodgeville win. Dick promptly stated, "I think Coach Wilson is the reason we won state. All the players had bought into his system, cared about each other, liked each other, and we had a great combination of skill, work ethic, character, and we complimented each other very well."

Some say Coach Wilson was ahead of his time with the construction of his defensive plan for North. Former Dodgeville and Hall of Fame coach Bob Buck, who followed Wilson at Dodgeville, had his own thoughts, "Coach Wilson once told me, 'Offense wins games, defense wins championships.' His game plan against Milwaukee North was the best I have ever seen in my life."

Recently, former Waukesha Coach Charlie Miller admitted to me what a serious misjudgment he had made of both the Dodgeville players and their coach prior to the North - Dodgeville matchup. North's full-court press had not presented the significant problem he had predicted for the Dodgers. This was an honorable gesture from a terrific coach.

North's Victor Anderson, who passed away on October 24, 2012, was an American in every sense of the word. As a Marine Raider, Anderson served our country in the Battle of Guadalcanal. He also saw action as part of the first wave of men to hit the beach on Iwo Jima and Guam, where they faced heavy resistance both times. In 1998, he was inducted into the Wisconsin Basketball Coaches Hall of Fame. He brought to his teams a strong sense of ethics and leadership. A few months ago I had the chance to speak with his son,

Victor, Jr., who as a fifteen-year-old viewed the title game from almost underneath the basket. "The referees seemed to be calling the game extremely tight, with some ticky-tack calls," he recalled. "Also, our players seemed to be lethargic. My dad had been in meetings all day and found out only after the game that the players had taken a long walking tour of the Madison campus and visited the Capital Building on game day, an activity he frowned upon and may have led to their sluggishness. However," added Victor, Jr., "You have to give credit to Dodgeville for their outstanding play."

According to North's Moton, after the game Coach Anderson told the Blue Devil's that it just had not been their night and gave Dodgeville due credit. On returning home from Madison, the Milwaukee North team was honored at a school assembly the following Monday. Blue Devil guard Tom Martin presented the state runner-up trophy to the school. High school commissioner John Kaczmarek awarded the city conference trophy to the team. They had a remarkable year finishing the season with a 24-2 record.

Winning a state championship is an incredible achievement. But for every team that holds this honor there are hundreds each year that have their own personal stories of disappointment, as did North. Unfortunately, their seasons end with a loss. As a high school player myself, I vividly recall the deep, lingering feeling of sadness, knowing that my season was done and high school career over. One minute you're playing with zeal, excitement, all the emotions of the moment. The next brings a sad sensation of disbelief.

Wilson trusted the starting five more than the others. Hadn't this quintet demonstrated a level of cohesiveness that had brought the team to the championship? Hadn't they faced championship-game pressure the year before? Others tell us that Wilson was rewarding the quintet for their trust, loyalty and leadership within his system, especially regarding the new defensive scheme he employed—a scheme so intricate that only these five could handle it. Others say that Wilson wanted to demonstrate his team's rare endurance and adherence to his game plan and that he *could* play only five and still capture a state championship. Still others pose: *Was* this a once-in-a-lifetime group hand-picked by fate? Did this group possess all the needed skills—from the purely physical element of talent developed by years of experience playing as children to a staying power perfectly nurtured and built by Wilson himself to reach this particular pinnacle of performance? Was Wilson, too, in some respect, simply acknowledging fate itself?

The answer to this question will never be known definitively, but those in the very heart of the matter—the players themselves—have their own takes. "I think Coach wanted the game so badly that he didn't want to take any chances," says Pat Flynn. "Only Wilson can answer that," Kramer Rock tells us. "I rationalize not being used/played in the championship final with the saying, 'You stick with the girl who brung ya to the dance.' Wilson likely felt the same way." There is Dick Stephens: "I think he trusted his five and didn't want to change anything or do anything to interrupt it." Bob Rock offers the lengthier explanation: "I'm not sure how or when this would have transpired during the game, but I surmise it would have been during a timeout near the end of the game—and I don't remember Coach's exact words, but it was something to the effect of, 'You five have not played the entire game all year. You deserve one. Get out there and finish this thing.' He would have said this just to the five of us as the huddle was breaking up. I don't think anyone else on the team heard this. Although it was a great way to finish off our high school careers, I've always felt bad about it. It would have been great for everyone on the team to play in that game."

Even after all the years,—yes, now fifty—people remember the night of March 21, 1964. It has been the subject of many conversations throughout the years. Mike Reilly, a 1964 graduate of Dodgeville was a member of the Dodger inaugural golf team of 1962. In addition, he was the basketball team manager his freshman year and went on to become president of the letterman's club. His brother Pat was captain of the 1962-63 Dodger basketball team, who finished second to Manitowoc. During Mike's last three years of high school he wrote for the *Dodgeville Chronicle*. In 1998, still working and writing for the *Chronicle*, he had the opportunity to attend the Wisconsin High School Basketball Coaches Association Hall of Fame induction of Milwaukee North's Coach Anderson some thirty years after that championship game. During his time at North, Anderson had nearly a 90 percent winning record. Mike related, "I introduced myself to him and stuck out my hand. He stuck his hand out and when he heard the word 'Dodgeville,' immediately pulled it back. He said, 'I won't shake hands with anyone from Dodgeville.' He laughed and shook my hand vigorously. Their star player Blanton Simmons was at the banquet with him, and I got to sit and talk with him. He said, 'Boy, you guys sure did a number on me.'"

There are many incredible stories about high school basketball that mark our great country and our heartland communities. Through the last twenty-seven years, I have been reminded repeatedly how this Dodgeville story has an almost eerie resemblance to the 1986 movie *Hoosiers*. The two storylines do coincide in some respects, but depart in others. To begin with, the *Hoosiers* story is not a true story. The famed Hickory High was a fictional school. Many suggest the movie was based on the 1954 Indiana state championship won by tiny Milan High from Indiana, but the facts don't entirely support this either. To draw broader appeal for the movie, the producers did not base it on a single historical story, but on Indiana high school basketball of the 1950's as a whole. Yet, most believe that the last-second basket by Jimmy Chitwood in the movie was an accurate recreation of guard Bobby Plump's famous last shot for Milan High in 1954.

On the other hand, the Dodgeville story is entirely true and stands on its facts. Let me cite a few examples comparing Dodgeville to the movie version of *Hoosiers*. Both teams were part of an all-in-one division tournament and both stories happened more than several decades ago. Both teams were in the heartland of the Midwest, Indiana and Wisconsin. Each pitted a small, rural white, small school playing against a black, largely-populated urban school, a true David versus Goliath matchup. Each story centers around an older coach who had previously been a United States Navy Chief Petty Officer before arriving at the school. Each coach was stubbornly set in his ways and demanded his players adhere strictly to his system. Each school attempted to get rid of the coach, who responded with a winning team and a state championship.

However, unlike imaginary Hickory High and true-to-life Milan High School, Dodgeville went undefeated. They did not have a star player like Bobby Plump but depended totally on a team approach to win. Not one of Dodgeville's players went on to play major college basketball. Milan had several. Milan's average margin of victory in their championship season was 15.5 points per game while Dodgeville's was considerably better at 31.5. Dodgeville Hall of Fame Coach Bob Buck notes this last bit of difference: "The 1963-64 Dodgeville team was runner-up the year before, and in my estimation I have never seen the smallest school in one division tournament be runner-up in one year and win it all the next. Milan, Indiana didn't do that."

To many folks in Indiana, tiny Milan's 1954 run to the title still stands as the greatest sports story ever to come out of the state. Bobby Plump went on to an outstanding career at Butler University in Indianapolis, then played for four years with the Oklahoma 66ers in the National Industrial Basketball League. Today his restaurant in Indianapolis' Broad Ripple section, an establishment cleverly named 'Plump's Last Shot,' offers a nostalgic look at Indiana basketball. I asked Bobby how it felt to make that final shot almost sixty years ago before that jam-packed crowd at Butler Fieldhouse. "Simply amazing," he recalls. "Something I will never forget—but something that will always remain second to the birth of my children."

Leaving Madison the night of the championship was a feat in itself. With well-wishers everywhere, it was difficult for the Dodger contingency to escape all the adulation. As the two Chevy Greenbrier vans carrying the team and coaches made their way out of Madison, other travelers joined in along the way on the two-hour, forty-mile trip home. With horns blaring, the caravan made their way through the towns of rivals like Verona, Mt. Horeb, Barneveld, Ridgeway and Blue Mounds. In each town there were folks lined up on the streets, some hoisting signs, all cheering as the Dodgers made their way through. In a number of the cities their fire trucks and ambulances blew their horns, flashed their lights and cheered as the champions rolled by. Despite the cold, friendly hands from the crowd reached out to the Dodgers to congratulate them. By the time the caravan made its way down highway 18-151 and reached the outskirts of Dodgeville, it was estimated to be eight miles long. In Dodgeville, every side street was filled with cars wedging their way into makeshift parking spaces. Over 3,000 adoring and cheering fans lined the streets of Dodgeville to honor the undefeated state champs.

It seemed everyone wanted to take part in the party atmosphere. Unable to attend the 1964 Dodgeville championship game, 1954 grad Eric Hagerup nevertheless wanted to be part of the town's celebration. So what did he do? He told me. "Living in Whitefish Bay, Wisconsin, I watched the game on TV. Late in the game, with victory assured, I jumped into my car and made the 140-mile trip to be part of the festivities."

Julie Weiskircher, long-time next-door neighbor of 1964 player Dick Stephens, left Dodgeville in 1960 to join the order of the nuns at Rosary College in River Forest, Illinois. Raised in Dodgeville, she knew all the players. In fact, three were her cousins. Hearing that the Dodgers had made it to the title game, she was caught between home-town loyalty and religious obedience. "I wanted so badly to hear the game, but I was a Dominican Student Sister," she recalls. "We weren't allowed to listen to the radio without permission, provided we could even find one! Illinois was unaware of this 'major event.' My only hope was to find a radio and tune in to a Milwaukee station, since our opponent was mighty Milwaukee North. Could a young nun pull this off? Not alone, that's for sure. I loved my voice teacher, a 'soloist' in more ways than one—she had a studio in the Fine Arts building, plus a state-of-the-art radio!" Julie's teacher invited her to listen. It would be their little secret. But, to complicate matters, the outside doors were locked at night. "I had to go through a tunnel between the dorm and the studio. I wouldn't allow myself to be frightened, though I always practiced voice during the day," she said. "The reception was sporadic, and even with my ear right up to the speakers the announcer's voice came and went. I caught all the excitement, tension, hope, and worry, though! All right ... time to pray, as I imagined everyone else from home was doing. I was not singing a solo! When the screams of victory reached Illinois, I was jumping up and down! Who could I tell? Who could I share this with? Now there's the rub!"

Dodgeville Library Director Vickie (Reynolds) Stangel, a 1970 grad, badly wanted to attend the big celebration after watching the game on TV with her family. Though ill with chicken pox, Vickie and her four sisters persuaded their parents to drive them to Dodgeville. They arrived early and found a great parking space among the sea of well-wishers. But sitting in the car parked on the street, they could offer only silent congratulations: Their parents insisted on not rolling the windows down. Vickie remembers wishing she could have shaken the players' hands.

It would be a busy night for Dodgeville's police. Chief "Tiny" Carroll met the procession as it entered the city and directed the vans to use Beckett Street to arrive at the old school. Just before their arrival, columnist Lew Cornelius from the *Capital Times*, accompanying the Dodgers in one of the vans, heard Corky Evans shout, "State champs! Yabba, dabba do!" capped by Pat Flynn's "Old Dogtown will roll tonight!" Then the entire bus broke into "We are the Dodgers, the mighty Dodgers!"

The caravan finally made its way to the Dodgeville grade school gym at approximately 11:30 for a spontaneous celebration. Here, before a jam-packed crowd standing shoulder to shoulder, Coach Wilson addressed the adoring crowd. After a five-minute standing ovation, he began by telling the crowd, "We'll be in there next year again." The crowd cheered loudly with approval. Shaking visibly with obvious emotion, Wilson thanked the fans for their support and praised the players for the outstanding defensive job they had done in holding the explosive North team to its lowest output of the year. He also suggested he was definitely due a big raise! He then planted a kiss on his wife's cheek and apologized to her for his absence, which brought even more applause. With all the arduous planning and preparation, he had hardly seen her in the three weeks of the tournament. Then he pulled out and read a telegram of congratulations from Governor Reynolds.

After words from Principal Orris Boettcher, Robert Campbell, president of the board of education and Bob McNeill, president of the chamber of commerce and several others, it was time to hear from the players. Corky Evans remarked, "We wanted to make the last game the best. I think it was." Bob Rock confessed, "It's a little hard to believe it. It's like a dream." Cracked Bruce Harrison, "You get so you think like Coach Wilson and anyone who can stand us guys has to be great. Coach put us in the right frame of mind." Rick Brown paid tribute to the vanquished Milwaukee North team, "The team we played tonight was the best we ever ran up against and they deserve a lot of credit." Pat Flynn declared, "It's sort of a dream yet. Hope nobody wakes me up."

Ed Edwards, then a sixth-grader, could not attend all the Dodgeville games. Too many were sold out. So his father would sometimes drive him toward Platteville to pick up the radio signal. The two would sit in the car and listen in. A long-time Dodger fan, he recalls vividly the grand reception in the old gym. "Lucky enough to get a seat, I was high in the balcony behind the basket. The place was absolutely electric. My heroes entered and spoke movingly to the overflow crowd. Like every kid in Dodgeville, I wanted to be them. From that moment I knew what I wanted to be. They shaped my life." A Dodger basketball, football, and baseball player, Edwards graduated in 1970, attended UW-Platteville, and then went on to teach social studies and coach basketball for thirty-eight years, twenty-five in Darlington.

For Coach Wilson it *truly* was a night for celebration. This championship was the zenith of a coaching career that nearly ended two years earlier from his heart condition. Feeling on top of the world, he put it, "Winning the championship and having my health back are all I can ask. And now I can go on coaching for another ten years or so."

It was now time to get the party started. A rock band from Platteville provided the honors. Dancing continued long into the night, as neither the police nor Wilson seemed too concerned about curfew time. The large party finally broke up about 1:30. Other smaller parties then took its place. As 1964 grad Nancy (Eichorst) Buck recalls, "My mother had bought a cake decorated with champions. The guys and their girlfriends sat around and talked about what the game had been like. I remember how much fun it was watching the team play for Dodgeville." Jayne Harrison, mother of player Bruce said this, "It was amazing how our town clung to our 1964 basketball team. Cities around us followed too, even the grandparents. It was a time of uniting with rivals." It was a celebration to remember. Recalls Bob Rock, "I wanted that night to last forever ... maybe because of the fear of not knowing what to do, where to go after the win and the celebration and thinking it is suppose to go on and on." Tom Brunker noting how Saturday's party celebration lasted such a very long time admitted, "After Saturday night, I didn't get home until Monday!"

The night turned out a little differently for Bruce Harrison, he explained. "After we won, Coach called my Dad and said, 'Tell Bruce to get his butt down to my house.' Coach used to call me by my nickname, 'Grasshopper,' but he never did after the championship game. When I arrived, I saw that Don Humbert (my now deceased father-in-law and Coach's best friend) was there, too. The three of us sat and watched the game films together." Bruce later told me that during the viewing, Coach Wilson couldn't help himself and pointed out several occasions where Bruce could have made better decisions during the game!

Dick Stephens has a vivid memory: "The very next

morning I remember my mom waiting for me when I got up to go to church. She was a very shy and simple lady, but that short walk to St. Joseph's Church was one of my most sensitive moments in my life, because I could just feel the pride oozing out of my mom. That was a very meaningful walk—one I will never forget, and not a word was said."

At the request of St. Joseph's Father Doran, the Catholic team members invited the Protestants to mass. These boys had been inseparable since seventh grade. The invitation was a long overdue one. This the priest knew, as he talked about the boys all the time.

Team member Bob Anderson told me that right after the championship game, the team was inundated by reporters. Wilson's last interview still sticks in his mind. He explained. "Weenie sat on one of the narrow benches in the locker room and I was immediately behind him. His voice was strained and raspy and he looked exhausted. But he was also enjoying the spotlight. He answered a couple of easy questions, and then took one from a reporter asking what his future plans might be. He looked at the floor and shook his head. 'I need to get more money. I'm not paid enough.' The reporters jumped on that with a chorus of: 'You deserve more! Why are they being so cheap? You are the best coach in the state.' And finally, 'We're going to help you with this.' True to their word, the story broke that Sunday morning with each reporter adding his own 'spin.' Some said that their sources told them that Dodgeville had offered Weenie a new contract. Others said that Weenie was being recruited by every high school in the state. Another story had him offered the head basketball coaching job at Marquette University in Milwaukee—a job that went to Al McGuire."

Anderson went on. "The story was to have an impact on my father and our home life for awhile. My Dad was Superintendent of Schools, a position that includes oversight of all of the functions of the school from chalk boards to library books. One of his main responsibilities was negotiating teacher contracts and salaries. We were in the eye of the storm. After a week or so, Weenie's pay story was no longer in the media's eye and it was relegated to the chatter in the local barber shops and bars. At the school level, there were some heated school board meetings. I don't remember the specifics of the outcome, but Weenie stayed in Dodgeville until he died. My dad maintained that this whole money business story soured his enjoyment of our winning the state championship."

The *Milwaukee Sentinel* came out with its All-Tourney team on Monday. Rick Brown and Pat Flynn of Dodgeville were first team, along with Esthetial Ford of North, Dave Battist of Waterloo and Dave Jansson of Manitowoc. Corky Evans made second team along with Simmons of North, Riege of Waterloo, Grainger of Waukesha, and Manitowoc's Sullivan. Dodgeville's Bob Rock made third team.

Monday at 3:00 p.m. brought a second celebration in the Dodgeville gym. On hand were students, faculty and the townspeople. Wilson, and others from Saturday night, addressed the crowd. Wilson told the crowd that the

gym. The room was so packed that children had to sit on the floor. The MC for the evening was local TV personality John Shimmerhorn. The main speaker was John Kotz, a former UW-Wisconsin All-American in basketball. He praised the basketball team for being gentlemen and giving one hundred percent effort all the time. Principal Boettcher remarked, "When athletes want something so badly, they eat it and sleep it, the rest of the school usually falls in with the same attitude." Recognition was given to all the teams for their accomplishments. For football, Coach Ray Heim drew praise for leading the team in his first year to its undefeated season of 8-0. Heim named Bob Rock honorary captain and Corky Evans the most valuable player. Rick Brown was cited for being named first-team AP all-state. Rick Brown was also cited as an outstanding track star for the season, which was not yet complete. Rick had taken first place in both the 440-yard run and the high jump in several of the spring meets. Tommy Martin was chosen MVP in wrestling by Coach Heim and Denny Thomas was named captain. (See the appendix for a complete listing of all team members.)

Rick Brown, Pat Flynn and Bruce Harrison were named tri-captains of the basketball team and Harrison was named MVP by Wilson. In defense of his choice Wilson said, "Bruce was an excellent leader. He had to decide what defense the opposition was using and to pattern our attack, and he had to keep getting orders from me." Corky Evans won the annual free throw award. MVP Bruce Harrison presented their manager, Bobby Campbell, with a "manager of the year" award. In jest, he told the crowd that the team had pooled all their money together. Then, Wilson did something out of the ordinary. Always planning ahead, he appointed Dick Stephens as next year's basketball captain. He stated, "We have good size next year and these boys can go as far as they want to. I had Stephens on the bench next to me all season and he'll be my captain next year. It'll be up to the boys and what they do this summer."

The Dodgers eventually did take in that Milwaukee Braves' game and were honored on the field on April 26th. Some 600 Dodgeville residents joined the Dodger players in a caravan to Milwaukee and enjoyed the game at County Stadium. Why was this particular day picked by the Braves? As a tribute to Dodgeville, the Braves were playing the Los Angeles 'Dodgers'! As 1964 team member Tom Schleck remembers, "One of the best events was going to County Stadium and being introduced to the crowd. We were able to go into the Braves locker room after batting practice. I remember it was pitched by a guy by the name of Hank Fisher and I met Joe Torre. Hank Aaron came in with a sweeping hand gesture (to shake hands) and said, 'the Dodgeville Dodgers' in a "stretched out" way. I will always remember that."

The next day, April 27, brought another basketball recognition dinner. The celebration addressed only the achievements of the state championship team for the 1963-64 season. It was held locally at Thym's Supper Club just north of Dodgeville. The featured speaker for the evening was Henry Jordan of the Green Bay Packers.

Later in the spring of 1964, basketball players Tom Schleck, Curt Anderson, Dan Stombaugh and Rick Brown were finishing the track season. Brown ended up winning the sectional championship in the 440-yard dash and was the runner-up in the high jump. Bobby Anderson, Craig Brue and Mike Collins were again honing their skills as members of the golf team under new coach Mr. Cook. Tom Brunker, Bruce Harrison, Dick Stephens, Larry Wagner, Bob Rock, Corky Evans, Steve Schroeder, Ken Johanning, Mike Gust and Kramer Rock were members of the baseball team again, coached by Wilson. The team finished the year with a 15-1 record, losing their first game in the state tournament to a powerful Sauk Prairie team by a score of 5-4, in 12 innings. Sauk Prairie would go on to finish second in the state. (See the appendix for a complete listing of all team members.)

Truly it had been a magical year. The numbers are more than impressive. For the three major sports at Dodgeville for 1963-64, the football team finished 8-0, the basketball team 26-0 and the baseball team 15-1. With many of the same athletes playing an integral part of all three teams, they amassed an incredible combined record of 49-1. Coach Wilson had overseen 41 of the victories and sustained the one loss. Dodgeville athletics was a team effort. The inordinate success of these squads was due to the hard work, dedication and teamwork inspired by all team members and coaches. Without the sweat and sacrifice of each, such a result could never have been achieved.

Dodgeville: Capturing Hearts

To this day, the basketball runner-up award of 1963 and championship award of 1964 sit snugly in the school's trophy case. With such acclaim from their finals loss in 1963 and their unexpected victory in 1964, Dodgeville has become synonymous with the underdog story. In Wisconsin "Dodgeville" has become a household word that conjures up fond memories of a brilliant and unforgettable moment in Wisconsin sports history. Says Corky Evans, "I feel very honored to be part of both years. Every time I go back to Dodgeville's gym, I go to the trophy case and look at the silver ball (1963) and the gold ball (1964) trophies."

Lastly, I am drawn to an article written by Clifford G. Ferris of the *Rhinelander Daily News* in late March, 1964 shortly after the Dodgeville victory. The article appeared in the *Dodgeville Chronicle*. The item reads in part, "The other night I watched as the Dodgeville high school basketball team rallied after a half-time scoring deficit to beat a heavily-favored Milwaukee North team for the championship of Wisconsin. And then I have seen, these last few days, the reporting of the rousing reception given the Dodgeville team as it returned to its home town. So far as I know, I haven't a single acquaintance in Dodgeville—in fact, I'm pretty hazy about any geography and if you asked I'd have trouble putting my finger on Dodgeville's location. But these days I am feeling a kinship for these people of Dodgeville. I'm sharing their pride in the performance of their high school team." Yes, this sense of kinship had spread across the state like wildfire. It didn't matter where one resided. It was the sense of pride that we could all share in. The Dodgeville Dodgers had captured the hearts of Wisconsin fans.

Chapter Ten

With the graduation of the class of 1964 and the passing of summer, Dodgeville settled into another school year in the fall of 1964. It had been rumored that Wilson was looking for a salary hike due to his latest success. Some say he felt he could do a similar job at a larger school. There was even talk of him moving up to the college level. Despite all the chatter, when the school year started he was still employed at Dodgeville. The football team finished with a respectable 4-3-1 record in Coach Heim's second season on the Dodger sideline. Soon excitement filled the air as basketball began. Wilson worked hard preparing the 1964-65 team, but it was no easy task to replace the starting five from a state championship team. The team started out slow, initially failing to click as a unit.

Early in the season junior Randy Jackson (class of 1966) had the scare of his life. He got to practice one day only to be told by Coach Wilson that he was off the team. "I asked him what I had done," Randy recalls. "He said, 'I saw you last Friday night smoking in a phone booth downtown.' I told him—it was not me. Coach told me I was done—to go to the locker room and change. I did. At home my father asked me what had happened. I told him. And then I got some friends together. Each night we went out looking. The next Friday we drove by the booth—and there he was, a kid similar to me in height, weight, and hair color, smoking and talking on the phone. I raced home, got Dad, went back to the booth. 'I call my girlfriend every Friday from this phone about this time,' the guy told us. We drove to Wilson's. Coach was unwilling to listen to me. Dad got very upset, and finally Coach gave in. 'You may be the state's best basketball coach, but you'd be a very poor father,' said Dad. 'My son needs an apology.' Coach never did offer me one. But on Monday I was back on the team, having missed one game."

As the Christmas season approached, eight graduated members of the WIAA 1964 championship team ventured back to Dodgeville for an alumni game against Dodgeville's current 1964-65 team. The game was nearly a sellout as the two teams jockeyed for bragging rights. With the alumni up by only a point at half, it appeared to be a tight game. But with some great teamwork and hot shooting, the returnees blew it open in the second half to win by a convincing score of 62-40. It was a real treat for all the Dodgeville fans to see their beloved former and current players. At the holiday break, the Dodgers held a 3-2 record. However, as the new year began, the Dodgers began to play with a new resurgence and vigor.

It was during this year that a new high school basketball rule allowed only a team captain to speak with an official. During one timeout at a home game, Coach Wilson asked captain Dick Stephens to question a call made by referee Gene Calhoun. Stephens did so. "I don't need to explain it to you, son!" replied the ref, who, as Stephens tells of it, "was being a complete jerk." He elaborated. "When I got back to the huddle, Wilson asked me what Calhoun had said. When I told him, Wilson promptly marched down to the far end of the gym to confront the man himself. From a distance, he appeared to be giving Calhoun a tongue-lashing! His finger was waving. His face and manner were those of a man very upset." But there was a mystery here. "Calhoun, who would later become the head of Big Ten officials, never called a technical on Coach Wilson. He did not even respond," Stephens tells of it. "And as Coach returned to the huddle, the crowd went wild, applauding him every step of the way. None of us had ever seen anything like it before. There was some kind of respect that the official had for Coach Wilson. Weenie was never intimidated by any official or any man I ever saw him interact with. He was the alpha dog and he was glad to let everyone know it."

The next 12 games saw the Dodgers turn up the heat and go 11-1. They seemed to be on a roll, but every game was vitally important, as the conference race was extremely tight. The Dodgers finished the season third in the conference and played their way into the sub-regional finals with a team that had been made up of substitutes from the 1963-64 team. Here they lost to their arch-rival and the eventual 1965 state champion, Monroe. The Dodgers final season record was 14-4.

That spring Wilson became the driver's-education teacher at Dodgeville. Three-sport athlete and 1967 grad Denny Rundle, who played football and basketball for Wilson, told me about being in his first driver's-education class. "There was a great deal of classroom work, but we spent many hours in the designated car as well, which had a brake on the right side for Wilson. Coach loved to take us over to Mineral Point because the city had an intersection where five streets met. Four of the streets had stop signs and only one, Highway 23, did not require a stop. To make matters worse, one of the stop signs was situated on the left side of the road. Here he would confuse us—who were so nervous to begin with. If that wasn't enough, he would roll down his window and whistle and heckle at passers-by. It was so embarrassing for us. This he knew, but he wanted to make us learn to concentrate on driving. It was all in fun— for him!"

Coach Wilson continued to coach basketball and baseball for the next four years and continued to meet with great success. He also went back to football in 1967 for a season after Coach Heim left. However, on October 30, 1968, tragedy struck the entire Dodgeville community. After finishing his normal morning routine of sweeping the gym floor in preparation for the day's physical education classes, Wilson discarded the broom, reached for a basketball and turned towards the court. Suddenly, he collapsed on the sideline, suffering another heart attack. He was found initially by students and CPR was administered by several teachers. This time he would not recover. He was pronounced dead by paramedics arriving on the scene. He was later taken by ambulance to St. Joseph's Hospital.

The news spread like wildfire. In a flash, their teacher, coach, and mentor was gone. He had meant so much to the school, the students, the community. So much was on the minds of so many people as they sought some rationale from above. Why, they asked, would he be taken from them at such an early age with so much more to give?

Dick Stephens, 1965 grad who was away at college, remembers first learning of his coach's death. "I remember coming back from class and my roommate Greg Szajna coming immediately down the stairs to tell me, 'Your Coach Wilson died today.' At UW-Whitewater, I had many people express their sadness at his passing."

Tom Stephens, Dick's younger brother and 1969 grad, was a senior at Dodgeville at the time. A three-sport athlete, he had played basketball and baseball for Wilson. He told me what transpired. "I was in the cafeteria when a student ran in and alerted the teachers who were there that Coach Wilson needed assistance. They hurried to the gym and I followed. I remember Mr. Cook and Mr. Walz and others working hard to revive him, without success." Tom continued, "The mood in the school that afternoon was gloomy. I can remember classmates quietly crying. As high school kids, we were numb with shock." Finally, he added this, "The seniors on the team for the upcoming season served as pallbearers for his funeral, as that was what he had requested his wife to do if something like this were to happen."

The day that Coach Wilson passed away, social studies/ English teacher Roger Hirstein was in the cafeteria. He heard the call for help and raced to the gym. "I found Coach on the floor, fighting to survive. I sent someone to the office to call for an ambulance," he recalls. "Coach looked at me as he continued his struggle. It was a terrible moment. Eventually the paramedics arrived, but it was too late." Wilson's basketball assistant for three years, Hirstein remembers the day that Wilson asked him to be his assistant coach. "I loved the sport but felt I really didn't know enough about it to help. 'Don't worry,' he told me. 'I'll teach you all you need to know.'" Hirstein was also the cross country coach. Wilson had started the program a year earlier and had asked Hirstein to take over. Hirstein explained, "Wilson had a rule that any potential basketball player who didn't play football had to go out for cross country, so when I took over the program I had forty guys show up at the start of the season. That really helped lead to the team's success. The team won the Wisconsin state championship in 1967 and never finished lower than fourth in the state in the four years I was the coach."

A wake for Coach Wilson was scheduled for Friday evening at Lulloff's funeral home. A special service would be held on Saturday morning at 10:00 in the school gymnasium. On Thursday the school had decided to postpone its Friday night football game with Cuba City to Saturday. Coach Bob Buck was asked to step in as basketball coach, as the season was to begin on Monday. Bob had to relinquish his duties as head coach of wrestling to do so. In addition, being head football coach, he had to coach Saturday's game with the death of his friend and colleague weighing heavily on his mind. Friday night's service for Wilson was heavily attended. On Saturday morning promptly at 10:00, Wilson's memorial service began. Nearly a thousand people were on hand for the open-casket service in the gymnasium, which included nearly the entire student body, teachers and most of the town's dignitaries. Together they would mourn their coach, a man Dodgeville would so dearly miss.

John "Weenie" Wilson was born in Richland Center, a small community located in Southwestern Wisconsin, on February 26, 1914. His parents were William and Ethelyn. His father was employed as a grocer and built his own store. John was one of seven children. There were three boys, John the oldest, William and Richard (Dick). The girls were Avenelle, Wilda, Phyliss and Jeanne. Avenelle passed away at nine months of age from meningitis.

Showing an early affinity for sports, John played football, basketball, baseball and track at Richland Center High School. As a senior, in 1933, he played in the WIAA State Basketball Tournament. He was inducted into the Richland Center High School Hall of Fame in 2000. But John isn't the only Wilson to be inducted there. Nancy (Robison) Tiegs, John's niece, and the daughter of his sister Jeanne, is a 2008 Hall of Fame member in gymnastics, track and volleyball. Through the years she remembers hearing stories of her uncle's playing prowess and coaching expertise. Nancy said, "My mom always told me I was the most like Uncle John because I would not drink alcohol no matter what. Also, because I was an athlete, PE teacher and I coached for years." Yet another Wilson, John's great-niece, 28-year-old Anne Wilson, was a standout in basketball at Richland Center High School. Anne is a 2012 Basketball Wall of Fame

Inductee at Viterbo University. At 6'1", she competed at the center position and set several school records in blocked shots and rebounds. On the all-time records list at Viterbo University, she currently ranks first in blocked shots, second in career points, and third in rebounds. Today, she teaches fourth grade in Richland Center and assists with the youth and high school basketball programs.

After a stellar career at Richland Center, John Wilson attended the University of Wisconsin-Madison. While punting during an intramural football game, the 5'7", 150-pound halfback was discovered by the late Clarence W. Spears. Spears was the head football coach at Wisconsin from 1932 to 1935 and enticed Wilson to come out for the team. At UW-Madison, it was said Wilson would consume a bowl of Wheaties almost every morning at Rennebolm's Pharmacy. He did this so often that his buddies began to call him "Wheaties." It was the following year in 1935 that Wilson joined the football team at Wisconsin. When Coach Spears first heard someone call "Wheaties" by his nickname, he thought for sure he had heard "Weenie" and the new translation stuck forever.

Spears commented on Wilson's chances of playing in the 1935 campaign as early practice began: "I don't suppose he will play regularly, but this John Wilson of Richland Center will see plenty of action or I miss my guess. He's got the face of a football player, and if that sounds silly, just ask coaches or veteran football judges if there isn't plenty in it. For another thing, he is fast and moves with a loose-hipped rhythm and grace that one always looks for in a natural ball carrier. He is a sophomore and as green as most sophomores, but he does many things instinctively that other players learn only from bitter experience." In 1935 Wilson lettered for the Badgers as a starting halfback. He also became a nationally-ranked punter and conversely returned one of the longest punts of his time.

I had the opportunity to speak with John's younger brother Dick, thirteen years his junior. Now 86, he still lives in Richland Center. Dick told me that from 1947-1949 he attended UW-Platteville. On weekends he would take a bus or even hitchhike to Dodgeville to see the Dodgers compete under the tutelage of his older brother. Sometimes he even got to sit on the bench. He took me back further, to the days when John played halfback and returned punts for Wisconsin. He told me that the entire family attended the Michigan game in 1935 when John took a reception from Wisconsin quarterback Lynn Jordan and raced 65 yards for a touchdown. What happened next is astonishing. On his way back to the bench, John thumbed his nose at the Michigan crowd. Not only was the crowd upset, but John's father, viewing the action, was irate. He immediately left his seat and after a few minutes made his way to the Wisconsin bench. There he vigorously scolded his son for his actions on the field. Dick told me it got so intense that the referees had to come over to break it up.

Wilson finished his final years of college at the University of Dubuque. Here he made all-conference in football and received national acclaim. He led the Spartans in scoring with 49 points on seven touchdowns and seven points after. He is credited with punt returns of 90, 73 and 70 yards. John, an incredible all-around athlete, also played two seasons of minor league baseball with the Williamson Colts in 1938 and 1939 where he was a teammate of Stan Musial.

Wilson joined the Green Bay Packers in 1939 for a brief period and then played a season with the Milwaukee Chiefs of the old American Football League. Late in 1939, during World War II, he decided to join the U.S. Navy, serving from 1939 until 1944. He rose to the rank of Chief Petty Officer, spending most of his enlisted time at the United States Naval Hospital in Bainbridge, Maryland. Here he worked to rehabilitate the returning war-injured. Receiving his honorable discharge in 1944, he finally decided to hang up his athletic ambitions as a player. He returned to the University of Dubuque to pick up some needed courses and was subsequently granted a physical education degree in 1944. He was then hired by Dodgeville High School as a physical education teacher and coach. During his tenure he coached baseball, football, basketball and one year of cross country.

His record was no less than stellar. His baseball teams won 10 conference championships and reached state on four occasions. His overall record was 166-42. In football, where he was a defensive specialist, Wilson compiled a 47-43-6 record amassing four co-conference championships. His basketball record of 359 victories and 141 losses includes

with the rest of us as our heroes. He made the playing fields respectable. Never by preaching or propaganda but by sheer contagion of his joy in so doing he made us want to play. In this regard he made us a people of better health and happiness in peace; of greater strength in adversity. This was his gift to Dodgeville; few men have made greater. People felt better in his presence. He made us all feel better - made us feel that somehow we could do more. This was his gift to his friends. He felt that courage was a major virtue; that all things work together for good to him who is unafraid. And the God of courage heard and gave him the last great reward that life can bestow - a sudden and painless and unexpected death. To believe that such a life is ended is to say that human life itself is meaningless and the universe a ghastly joke. No one of us believes that. Coach Wilson is not lost to us. We are all going to heaven, and Coach is there already, telling his stories, talking his wisdom, cracking his jokes, and, we may be sure, encouraging play. Already they have learned to love him. And he is waiting for us - still with his joy of living and his eternal courage."

Neal Nelson, a 1973 Dodgeville grad and Dodgeville and Wisconsin Hall of Fame coach, experienced Wilson's death as a grade-schooler. He remembers, "When Coach Wilson died, I was in eighth grade and it was devastating. I remember being at the memorial service held in the packed gymnasium. I got so emotional. I was sitting next to Mark Schroeder, who became the basketball coach at Plainfield High School and he was crying hard, too. We already felt him in our souls. In my office I have always had the 1964 Dodgeville team picture on the wall along with a Green Bay Packer picture of Coach Wilson sitting between Curly Lambeau and Don Hudson. I love telling my players about the Dodgeville *Hoosier* story."

Florence Crubaugh, Dodgeville resident and sister-in-law of John Crubaugh, was a great friend of Coach Wilson and his wife, Blanche. She explained, "Blanche went to the funeral at school with Eva (her mother) and some of Coach's family. I stayed home to look after their house and helped with the food and Blanche's needs. Many people were dropping off sandwiches and hot dishes for Blanche, to be of help in her grieving."

Royce Reukauf taught history and driver's education at Dodgeville in 1968. In addition, he served as Wilson's JV football coach for three years. In his time at Dodgeville, he said that he found Wilson to be a very serious individual. Royce was in attendance at the funeral and told me recently that the memorial was held in the gym with an open casket and it was well-attended with many coaches and former players present. Royce said Wilson's death took us all by surprise, and was a sad day for Dodgeville.

Even today, people still embrace Coach Wilson and are saddened by his sudden death at such an early age. At age 90, Bill Singer, a Dodgeville native and founder of Singer Lumber, recently noted, "If Weenie had been exposed to some of today's heart procedures, I'm quite sure he would not have died a young man."

189

Not long ago Coach Buck told me about how chaotic it was with the town grieving, having to coach the football game and give the eulogy for his friend Coach Wilson, all within days. "Wilson came and found me at school on the Monday before his death," he recalled. "He congratulated me on the big victory over Mineral Point on Friday night. Point was predicted to win, but we beat them." He continued, "Wilson was very excited as he was scheduled to go deer hunting the next weekend and he could hardly wait. John loved to deer hunt." I asked Coach Buck about the difficulty of leaving wrestling and taking over the basketball program on such short notice. He replied, "About half of the kids I taught in grade school and many were on the football team. The toughest part for me was going from the figure four (wrestling move) to the figure eight (basketball drill) and keeping them straight!"

I caught up with Chuck Tank, who retired as Dodgeville basketball coach in 2009. Still teaching history, he told me that he arrived in Dodgeville amid some very unique circumstances. After coaching basketball for five years in Plymouth, Wisconsin, five years in Alliance, Nebraska and one year at St. Mary's in Fond du Lac Springs, he accepted the Dodger head position in 1990. Upon Coach Wilson's death in 1968, Coach Buck had stepped in, until he retired in 1985. Then Gary Olson took over the program, but in his second year he was diagnosed with health issues and chose to step down. In 1988, Dave Grunow accepted the coaching position. During Dave's second season, former Coach Gary

Olson died. Months later, with his team playing in the first game of the post-season against Prairie du Chien, Grunow himself suffered a heart attack and was rushed from the locker room to the hospital by ambulance. His players decided to finish the game for him and ended up losing a game that went down to the wire—as he lost his fight for his life. Under such sad circumstances, Coach Tank stepped in, and the Dodger lineage continued. Coach Olson's son was a member of Tank's first team at Dodgeville.

Ever since the Wilson era, guiding the program has been no easy task. I asked Coach Tank what it was like for a first-year coach to take over. "When I came to Dodgeville in 1990, it was not an easy transition," he explained. "Many community members were hungry to return to the glory days of 1964."

Scott Von Rueden, who played for Coach Tank, is a 2002 Dodgeville graduate. His father Ken runs the feed mill once owned by the father of 1964 player Bob Rock. Scott competed in football, basketball, and baseball for the Dodgers and went on to play baseball at Edgewood College. I asked Scott about the 1964 team, and about the Dodgeville tradition. "Having a *Hoosiers* tale in your own town is incredible," he told me. "Most likely that team did establish the tradition we have today. But as a kid, you remember what you see. The 1993-1995 era of the Borne twins, Brett and Brad, was my introduction. Two close losses to Auburndale in 1993 and then in 1995 kept us from advancing at state." Each new team adds another layer, another bank of memories. Collectively,

suitcase, including her prized antique mirror she loved so much, and head to a Greyhound bus stop. She would take the bus to Lake Geneva where her mother lived. This happened several times and she always seemed to get the same bus driver each time. One time, as she was getting on the bus, the driver exclaimed, 'Little lady ... you should either figure out a way to get along with him or get yourself a smaller mirror!'"

Florence added, "After Coach died Blanche was extremely sad as it was very hard to get along without him. She didn't go to games anymore. As a means of socializing she took a job at the Ben Franklin store on Main Street in Dodgeville. Her sister Maxine, who lived in California, tried to talk Blanche into moving to nicer weather. Eventually, as Blanche's health deteriorated, she did go live with Maxine." Blanche Wilson passed away on May 1, 1994 at the age of 77.

It took years for the community to get over the loss of Coach Wilson. Even today, the basketball style of uniforms and the manner of play may be different, but the memories and the love of the game are still present in Dodgeville. The legacy left by John Wilson is still alive and continues to be shared by all. It will be forever. Dodgeville was always a city rich with pride, but the influence of Coach Wilson augmented that pride insurmountably. Perhaps in some way it was more than fitting that Wilson died in his own special place in Dodgeville, the place where for so many years he brought fans to their feet and glory to the Dodger faithful. Today there is a plaque in the Dodgeville gymnasium honoring Coach John D. "Weenie" Wilson. It tells about Wilson's accomplishments and what he contributed to Dodgeville High School through his twenty-four years of service. Among those attributes is a citation Wilson received from the Wisconsin State Legislature for having an outstanding, disciplined team and record in 1964 as noted earlier. In the early 1970s the Dodgeville Athletic Field was renamed Wilson Park in honor of Coach Wilson. His good friend, Bob Buck, was a member of the JC's committee that helped enact that change.

There are others who have Wilson's vision and spirit. James (Joe) Whitford, 1964 assistant coach, left Dodgeville at the end of the school year to continue his career in Waterford, Wisconsin. Whitford was assistant boys basketball coach at Waterford from 1967-1976. I was extremely surprised to find out that I, myself, had played against Coach Whitford during this period of time, when I was a student at Kettle Moraine High School in the late 60's. No doubt I shook his hand numerous times after games, as Waterford was a member of our conference, the Southeastern Badger. In 1977, Coach Whitford took over the Waterford girls' program where he compiled a record of 155-45, winning the Class B state championship in 1985. After his victory, he remembered his Dodgeville days and planned a similar tribute to his team's title win. Upon their arrival back home in Waterford, he requested that there be fire trucks out to greet the girls and celebrate the victory. There they were, right on cue! A few months back I had the opportunity to speak with Coach Whitford's daughter Julie (Whitford) Seidel about her father. Recalling her own Dodgeville days, Julie told me, "The night of Dodgeville's 1964 state championship victory, my sister, brother and I were home sick with the measles in Dodgeville, unable to attend the big game. In an effort to allow my mother to attend the game, a neighbor, out of the kindness of her heart, came over and watched us girls." Julie had one more significant item to point out. "My dad built the original signs on the outskirts of the city that read 'Welcome to Dodgeville - Home of the 1964 State Basketball Champions.' He did this with the help of his industrial arts students."

In February, 2004, forty years after the incredible victory, the 1964 championship team was reunited back in Dodgeville to be introduced during half-time of a basketball game. For many Dodgeville people, memories seemed to spill out. Neal Nelson, who was himself inducted into the Wisconsin Basketball Coaches Association Hall of Fame in 2012, was on hand for the event. Neal, who grew up and played for Coach Buck in Dodgeville, is the winningest men's basketball coach in Wisconsin junior college history after a 30-year career at UW-Waukesha. His teams won over 500 games, 5 state championships and 16 conference titles. Neal believes it was the 1964 State Championship basketball team that inspired him to become a basketball coach. Neal gave me his sentiments about the evening. "On a cold January night, I was more than happy to make the two-hour drive from Waukesha back to Dodgeville to see this. When the players came out of the locker room to be introduced, it was like being in the movie *Field of Dreams*. To see my heroes come out of the cornfield was a thrill." Bruce Harrison, an honored member from the 1964 team, spoke with Neal individually after the introduction. The occasion must have jogged memories of Harrison's playing days. Neal related, "Bruce said in one game he took a bad shot right before half-time. Coach Wilson went totally Woody Hayes or Bobby Knight on him!"

In early 2010, Dodgeville teacher Jeff Bradley created a Dodgeville Hall of Fame, an idea stemming from efforts at earlier school meetings to build school tradition. A committee was formed of a variety of community residents with ties to Dodgeville athletics. The Hall is financially supported by the DHS Athletic Booster Club and serves to honor those individuals for significant achievements at Dodgeville. Jeff explained further. "The goal is to establish a new tradition and let the kids know a little about the past here in Dodgeville. So many graduates have left here and gone on to be very successful in their lives." He further demonstrated its impact. "I think it's important for students to realize that what they do here can leave an impact on a lifetime—whether it's athletic or academic. They can see that others have worked hard, excelled and left their mark, and they have the opportunities of doing that, too." Jeff spoke from his personal experience. "When I go to the state tournament people still talk about the 1964 team when they see me wearing some things that say 'Dodgeville Basketball.' People say 'Oh, I remember watching those guys at the Field House ....'"

In October, 2010 Dodgeville inducted 22 members as its charter hall of fame class. Among them were 18 individuals and four coaches. This group included six individuals from the 1964 state championship basketball team. In addition, the entire 1964 basketball team was honored. Recognized were Archie Hahn, Butch Perkins, Forrest Perkins, Chuck Halverson, Ross Vivian, Harold Chappell, Dick Rundle, Dennis Morgan, Bruce Harrison, Bob Rock, Corky Evans, Patrick Flynn, Rick Brown, Dick Stephens, Vince Lease, Karri Roh, Regina VanDyck and Brett Borne. The coaches honored included John Wilson, Julie Van Epps, Pat Reilly (Coach/Athlete), and Bob Buck.

Created in 1998, the Dodgeville Area Scholarship Fund, Inc. (DASFI) offers more educational opportunities to Dodgeville grads. Currently Missy Hottmann is its president. The main fundraiser for DASFI is the annual golf outing held each year on the third Sunday in September. Here, alumni gather at Dodge Point Country Club for an enjoyable day of golf and fundraising to benefit Dodgeville's upcoming graduates.

Bob McGraw was a lineman for the Dodgers' 1963 undefeated football team. Called quiet, a bit shy, kind, and a great teammate, Bob contracted cancer at the end of the 1963-64 school year and passed away in November, 1964. One of the teammates at his funeral, 1965-grad Dick Stephens, recalled a young girl there, perhaps a younger sister. Years later, at the inaugural golf outing, Dick saw a familiar face selling raffle tickets and asked who she was. Sure enough, it was Bob's sister Milly (McGraw) Babcock, a 1971 Dodgeville grad. Milly, a DASFI board member at the time, was auctioning two pies baked by her 91-year-old mother Kathryn, herself a Dodgeville grad. The last few years Milly's sisters Margaret and Diane have helped with the baking. These two pies can fetch $300-$400 each. Milly and her sister Diane will then cut and serve the pies to the top bidders, a group of 12 or so guys from that era who pool their money each year to get the pies. Involvement in DASFI and the golf outing has been a way for the McGraw family to bond and give back to a community which had been their rock years before. "Meeting Dick Stephens, Bill Rock, Kramer Rock and Bobby's classmates from years ago brought wonderful memories to my mom and siblings," Milly told me. "To reconnect with Bobby's teammates has been a special gift, bringing much joy to our family. It keeps Bobby's memory alive." Another brother Pat, whose Dodger cross country team won the state championship in 1967, is a Hall of Fame member.

This past fall the 1963 football team received a long-overdue honor. On its 50th anniversary, the 8-0 team was inducted into the Dodgeville Hall of Fame. The entire McGraw family was in attendance for Bob's induction.

We have now reached the milestone of fifty years since the 1964 basketball championship. Through the years the trees of success planted by Coach Wilson have grown and matured. One of these is a tree of coaches. That so many of his players and assistant coaches have gone on to become highly recognized coaches in both high school and college sports is a tribute to the values and sheer love of sport that Wilson instilled in Dodgeville. Moreover, many of his players who chose not to pursue athletics any further have gone on to successful professional careers directed by many of his guiding principles.

To this day the '64 team members have stayed the best of friends and communicate and visit each other regularly. There are numerous reunions. Their life-long friendships include the cheerleaders and other classmates as well. After all, these students and the entire school were there to provide the needed support that propelled the Dodgers forward. Without the lettered signs, enthusiastic cheers and generous support of the Dodgeville student body, the 1964 victory might never have been possible.

Larry Wagner, 1964 team member, passed away in 2010. His wife Marcia told me about Coach Wilson and the Dodgeville camaraderie. "Coach Weenie Wilson was a tough coach and expected a lot from the athletes, but Larry looked up to him and admired what he taught them all. The guys from the teams have stayed very close and got together several times through the year either at a sporting event or on a golf course. Because of their success, they are more like brothers/family, and I am still in contact with many of the guys."

Mike Collins, another '64 team member, sums it up well: "One thing that was gratifying was how the starters treated the rest of us at reunions. We all had matured and they didn't seem so elitist. They expressed gratitude for the parts the rest of us played and seemed to recognize we all played important roles in our success."

The 1964 team was, so to speak, an unusual group. One of its most important characteristics was the "family" feeling of unity as demonstrated by their play. This is no accident. Several Dodgers are not only "team" brothers but cousins by blood. Corky Evans is related to three players (Bob Rock, Kramer Rock, and Bruce Harrison) as a first cousin, and one other player (Dick Stephens) is his fourth cousin by great-grandparental sisters. Corky is related on both his mother's and father's sides. Four other players are related, but only on one side. These connections certainly would help instill the loyalty which family demands. Eleven of the fourteen team members went on to graduate from college. All but five stayed residents of Wisconsin. The group has remained great friends through the years. It is a friendship built on love and trust.

Chapter Eleven

Many times success and winning can reveal our characters and conceal our shortcomings. A basketball team may have an incredible night and shoot 70 percent from the floor and earn a close win against a great team. Accolades will come their way and their coach will be held in high esteem. Sometimes, unfortunately, enthusiasts look only at the end result. It is human nature to do so. But what if in this same contest the winner had been severely out-rebounded, or committed numerous turnovers but their opponent had suffered a poor shooting night, or had played without its best player? Here one might question the quality of the victory. In other words, if these same two teams met again, the result might be vastly different. This is why delving into detail is important. Despite victories, close analysis can uncover a team's flaws and weaknesses. This is why, in a sport so uncontrollable, many coaches stress *defensive effort*—a variable they believe they can control. Then, might it be possible to conceive that even Dodgeville had a weakness?

When we peer at the Dodgeville yearbook for 1963-64, we see the words VENI, VIDI, VICI. These words (I came, I saw, I conquered) were originally spoken by Julius Caesar in 47 BC in his commentary regarding the Roman campaign in Britain. Dodgeville, too, used these same words to describe the 1964 year of basketball highlights, their conquests and their final crowning as state champion. But unknown to many, Wilson, like Caesar, had a group plotting against him, a number of members from the Dodgeville School Board.

Coach Wilson's teams met with great success. His record as a coach was incredible. He was a master coach in many, many ways. At the same time, like most coaches, he had his critics. In the summer of 1962 several school board members were ready to oust Wilson from his coaching position, prior to the 1962-63 season. The powers-to-be claimed he was not a "tournament coach." A closer examination indicated there may have been other glaring issues at the heart of the matter. Some thought he was too tough and overbearing. He got good results, but at what cost? His sometimes-harsh style may have been understood by some but was a deterrent to others. He may have been cordial off the court, but a brutal force in the gym. He had treated many a referee in a harsh manner that some viewed as disrespectful.

Coach Wilson used an authoritarian style of coaching as evidenced by his beliefs and behaviors. Reasons for this choice may be due to his unique experiences as a child, a player, an assistant coach or perhaps a coach. Many coaches see themselves as authority figures. Some have a need for control, and coaching meets that need. Many feel that, in stressful situations, a take-charge person is a must. Many coaches do not know or care to understand other styles and may be unable to delegate. Still others may feel that harshness is the only way to make a point. Sometimes the authoritarian style can go too far and yield an outcome that can approach a "third-rail" of coaching. Here coaches may go beyond the norm physically and/or emotionally, resulting in visible player-coach tension. The consequence of such behavior can result in a team's having emotional highs and lows which can breed inconsistency. Maybe it is pride, desire or pressure to win, or only a teaching moment from a coach's perspective. In a nutshell, it is a time when a coach can allow emotion to trump logic.

This third-rail topic was the concern of the school board, but like most controversial issues, it was very difficult to discuss, especially in public. Some did feel that Wilson overstepped his bounds to the detriment of players and referees. At the same time, Wilson's teams were adept in fundamentals, consistent, intelligent and winners. His players were model students. The paradox hinged on this very-charged issue that seemed to some degree readily apparent to all. Back in the 1960s, this style of coaching was the way of many. Wilson, like many other war veterans, had a spot-on understanding of the need for leadership in any organization, stemming from his military involvement. This background aided Wilson and others to develop their tough approach to life. In the armed services, the need for survival was far more real than at a high school sporting event. For Wilson, he did things his way, the only way he knew and the only way he truly believed would breed success. In his view, he was teaching his boys responsibility and taking care of his program properly.

Strong-minded kids with hard-working values, too often without question yielded to Wilson's vision and authority. In the 1960s, coaches and teachers were viewed as superior beings not to be questioned, especially if they were successful and winners. That's just the way it was. Wilson forever wanted the best for his players, academically and athletically. His personality worked for many, but not for others. His "my way or the highway" approach stood between many a player who loved sports and knew very well they must go through this man and this man only to pursue their love of sport at Dodgeville. After all, Coach Wilson was the great gatekeeper and ran football, basketball and baseball for many years. A player who angered this coach might as well give up all these sports.

In the 1960s and even today, parents can be brutally honest and emotionally critical. They use this rationale as a reality check for their child. In other words, they stand in direct alignment with a coach who believes that a player learning his shortcomings at this critical stage in his maturity brings about a positive outcome. Consequently, many of the Dodger players thought nothing of Wilson's philosophy. It didn't seem out of the ordinary and besides it was meant to put them on the proper track. His tough-love approach made great sense as they received much the same at home. Wilson had instituted a curfew, and expected citizenship from his players. Those were positives for the parents, too. Earl Williams, a 1955 Dodgeville grad, played under Wilson and went on to officiate more than 7,300 ball games at various levels of sport. He related, "Wilson was very vocal, and would have a problem today. I got pushed around more than once by him. As a kid, I had no problem with it; that was the way it was."

However, a few of the parents considered their school's coach simply to be out of control. Others honestly did not see the virtue in Wilson's philosophy and questioned its application in the long run. Many parents who are eager to support their child, even when he was unable to make the grade in a sport or activity, are quick to blame. Too often this meant that coaches get extra scrutiny and are unjustifiably held to account. Parents want the best for their child but many times over-parenting can yield an opposite result. Allowing a child to fail on their own can help develop needed coping skills.

Most coaches seem to think that 'who better to judge the players than themselves, the ones that see them perform day in and day out.' Wilson was a "tell it like it is coach" who, without question, treated all of his players the same. But with different family backgrounds, philosophies and parenting styles, not all parents saw a level playing field. In some people's eyes, a calmer, more emotionally caring coach would have been a healthier choice for Dodgeville.

Supporting these conspirators were stories about Wilson, even as early as the junior-high level. Eric Hagerup, a 1954 Dodgeville grad and athlete, whose own dad passed away early in his life, saw Coach Wilson as a substitute father. He recalls his first encounter with the man. "I was in my first sixth-grade PE class with about twenty other students. As the class started, Wilson told us all to line up on the basketball court sideline. 'Look at me. Face me. Dress right, dress!' he barked. Hearing this military command, one boy started laughing. Wilson stepped over, snatched up the youngster and carried him to the swinging doors adjacent to the gym. He then tossed him through, leaving the doors swinging back and forth. The gesture left a lasting impression. It was the last time anyone questioned his authority."

Coach Wilson did however have a milder side at times. When he was not on the field, court or diamond his demeanor could change significantly. Kramer Rock describes one such occasion. "We actually did meet at the pool hall before away games. Coach mandated departure time and God love you if you were late. Coach waited for no one. When it was time for the bus to leave, you better have your duffle bag and raggedy butt in a seat or you were left. Miss the bus and you were on his 'hit list' forever. We'd mosey in prior to the departure time. We'd sit around antsy, equally excited and bored. Coach would actually become human there. He had heart issues my sophomore, junior and senior years. He was taking some medicine for his heart at the time. It was in this setting I actually experienced a side of Coach I hadn't known, as one of his players. There was a human side, a sad side, fearful-of-dying side. He was not 'Coach' in those times, he talked to me one on one, as a young man. It was almost as father and son. I remember the moments vividly. They were too few and too fleeting. He was human. Those few moments are still positive memories of Coach Wilson."

All players want to play and contribute to the success of the team, but at the same time they are competing with their teammates for court time. Starters on a basketball team feel great about rising to that level. As a result, they feel a sense of loyalty to the coach for honoring them with their role. The starters certainly do not want to upset the apple cart, but subs don't want to remain on the bench forever. Usually the starters are leaders and the rest of the team yields to their direction, a form of peer pressure. At Dodgeville, all of the players were subject to the same close scrutiny of performance, thus yielding a team in which each player earned his position in the pecking order. There were no favorites in *this* respect.

In the summer of 1962, an emergency meeting was held at St. Joseph's grade school to prevent Wilson's dismissal as coach. The parish priest, parents, players and many Wilson supporters were on hand and formed a coalition to protect him. I asked John Crubaugh, a 1962-63 assistant coach, to explain what happened. "Several of his former players went to meet with the board members personally and as a group. I think I was the coordinator of our group. Eventually the board capitulated so John Wilson could return as coach." Crubaugh went on to tell me about his personal dealings with the board. "In the interviews I had with the board members, during the summer of 1962, they always mentioned that 'Weenie' wasn't a tournament coach. Never did any board member mention how he treated his athletes. Not once!"

Was it that the board didn't want to let its true intentions be known? Could publically addressing this third-rail issue carry a political cost? Might anyone who dared to broach the subject invariably suffer openly at the hands of the others?

How baffling was all this? Clearly, the focus of the School Board's accusation was on how Wilson interacted with his players.

Unlike Caesar's, Wilson's 'Ides of March' crisis turned out to be favorable. He was kept on in his same role at Dodgeville. He promptly responded to his critics loud and clear by finishing second in the state basketball tournament that year and with a state championship the next. In seemingly a flash, what many had viewed as a low point in the Wilson era appeared to boomerang to an incredible high.

Eli Crogan is a member of the Wisconsin Basketball Coaches Association Hall of Fame. In 42 years of coaching he amassed a 562-351 career record with stops at Soldiers Grove, Fennimore, Watertown, and Wayland Academy. In addition, he was head coach at UW-Whitewater for four seasons and scouted for the Houston Rockets of the NBA. Crogan is currently the mentoring director for the WBCA and has written a mentoring manual to help coaches succeed. He mentors coaches on an array of issues. Had his program been in place in 1962, he may have interceded at Dodgeville. I asked Eli what he felt were the three most important traits a coach could have. He replied, "relating to the players, knowing the game and being a good teacher." When coaching at Fennimore High, Eli went head-to-head with Wilson. I inquired what it was like to coach against Wilson back in the day. Eli told me, "To coach against Weenie Wilson you had to be well-prepared. Every possession was a battle. His players always played hard. Weenie had a way of working the referees." I then asked what he thought of the 1964 victory by Dodgeville over North. Said Eli, "Tremendous win for small schools. It was like it couldn't be done, but they did."

Wisconsin's own Dick Bennett, with a college coaching record of 489-307, was interviewed by Tim Froberg of the *Green Bay Press Gazette* in April, 2013. In light of last spring's national controversy involving a coach and players at Rutgers, one of Bennett's past employers, UW-Green Bay, had launched an investigation of its own. Bennett shed some light on the situation. "I think it's harder to coach today, without question," said Bennett. "The scrutiny is much greater. People will voice their disagreement or complaint much more readily, and, of course, it's publicized to a much greater extent than it was when I was coaching. The last ten years have brought a different, more intense focus on coaches and athletes." In regards to Rutgers and UW-GB Bennett, said, "There is no excuse for physical abuse. That's where the line has to be drawn. But sometimes people take offense at something that's said in the heat of the moment. As coaches, we've all gone right up to that line where we're angry and have said something that we regret. I would hate to hold a coach responsible for everything he said."

This new wave of reporting could alter coaching techniques and methods dramatically. "As long as it keeps getting reported, coaches are going to have to change," said Bennett. "But I think they're going to lose something in the process if all you can do is mollycoddle kids and tell them how great they are and not get to the point of, 'Hey, you're not getting the job done, you need to shape up.' We used to say, 'Let's keep it here,' but that doesn't happen all the time either. It gets outside of the circle of the team family and someone gets it and takes it out of context, and the next thing you know, you're on the carpet." Although Bennett is referring to the college basketball landscape, many of his points apply to the high school level and are pertinent in how coaches today are evaluated.

How we measure a coach can simply be determined many times by the way others view him. Many of Wilson's former players, some of whom went on to outstanding coaching careers of their own, were more than willing to step up and address their relationship with their former coach. Of Wilson, 1962-63 team captain Pat Reilly added, "He was the nicest guy you ever wanted to meet off the court and was no doubt the best competitor ever on the court. Maybe playing football at UW and with the Green Bay Packers along with some baseball for the St. Louis Cardinals, helped him make us the best we could be. I always considered it a great honor to play for him."

I caught up by telephone with 1964 player Rick Brown. Rick was deep in the woods extracting maple syrup from trees on a Wisconsin farm his great-great-grandfather had homesteaded right after the Civil War. I asked Rick about Wilson's lessons of tough love. "He was extremely tough, but we all bought in," he told me. "I knew he really cared about us. When I was sick with mono my junior year, he came to my home every noon hour and sat in the chair beside me, just to make sure I was okay."

Tom Schleck, 1964 team member shared his view. "Wilson ran very hard practices. He got us in shape to play a full game with energy. I think he was very good at teaching the fundamentals of basketball wherein the players understood what needed to be done in all circumstances. When watching basketball games today, I find myself almost screaming 'Don't let him drive the baseline' or 'Move the ball against the zone, don't dribble,' or 'Don't let them get a lay-up without paying for it.' He was excellent at 'game-planning' the opposition. Where I fault him is he wasn't a 'team' guy. There was the first five or maybe the first seven and then there were the rest of us. We were 16- and 17-year-old males with our own self-interests. Wilson was an adult and should have managed to build a team spirit where individuals operated for the team and not themselves. He knew how to coach basketball but not build a team."

Starting guard Bob Rock added this, "Weenie was tough. He was Dodgeville's own Bobby Knight. He ruled, and motivated by fear. I was afraid of him ... and cried at the supper table at home more than one night during my junior year. I think by the time we were seniors, our skins had grown a little thicker. He had thrown towels, clipboards on the floor during the game—not always angry at the refs but at one of us players. He wouldn't be able to keep a coaching job in a small town today, but things were different then and he was winning, so he had the support of parents and administrators."

Dick Stephens, a 1964 team member and 1965 team captain said this: "Coach Wilson seemed to have a love-hate relationship with some. For me he was one of the 'most influential people in my life.' He was hard to play for, as his expectations were unwavering and he was tough as nails. I always worked pretty hard at everything, but he loved to 'keep pushing me.' He told me one time, 'Notice that I am not yelling at all your teammates—it is when I stop yelling at you or expecting you to do something, that you should worry.' I took this to mean that he 'cared' about me, knew I was someone who could lead, was a good 'team' guy. Some hated his ways; not me, I loved his ways, even though it was hard. I always tell those that seem to not feel strongly about him, 'What would our lives have been without him?' I always feel blessed he was our coach. He had a great hand in all our successes."

Ronald Murphy played football under Wilson in the late 50s. A 1959 Dodgeville grad, he went on to play football at Platteville. He then coached football at Mineral Point for 32 years. I asked Ronald about his relationship with Wilson. "I played baseball for Coach Wilson from 1956-1959. During the baseball season, he would give my brother and me a ride home sometimes after practice," he told me. "We lived five and a half miles out of town on a farm. I played football under Wilson in 1958. He made it very clear what everyone's assignment was. Players that didn't play their position were told in no uncertain terms what they should have done. I followed a lot of his defensive principles during my 32 years of coaching football. His and my motto were the same— 'Keep it simple. Don't give up the big play.' I was a student teacher in physical education under Coach Wilson in 1964. One thing he stressed to me was, 'Be firm, but be fair to the students.' It was my pleasure to see him coach Dodgeville to the state championship in 1964. During my junior and senior years of playing football at UW-Platteville, Coach Wilson represented my father, who had passed away, on Parents Day. While attending college, Coach Wilson hired my brother and me to be referees for J.V. basketball games at Dodgeville. These are examples of the kind and generous person Coach Wilson was. He was like a <u>father</u> <u>figure</u> to me."

I asked 1963 player Bill Polkinghorn about Wilson's coaching style. "Discipline," he replied. "Not only on the court, but he carried it over to the classroom and social life. It is great if you can do it. You need the support of the community."

Yes, Wilson certainly did carry it over into the classroom. Ross Vivian, a 1950 grad who played under Wilson, remembers how "the principal would send anyone who got in trouble to Weenie." Apparently Wilson's reputation preceded him, and in this regard was actually a *blessing* to some Dodgeville administrators!

John Crubaugh, a 1962-63 assistant coach and 1957 Dodgeville grad played for Wilson. He went on to coach at both Cuba City and Tomah. I asked John what he learned from Wilson as both a player and an assistant coach and if Wilson had a sense of humor. John filled me in: "I learned a lot about basketball from him that made me a better coach. Unfortunately, I also learned things that I never wanted to follow about treating my players. I learned very little about life, about compassion for others, and even about appreciating their talents and interests. He did not possess a sense of humor. He carried at least a love-hate relationship with some players. He was hard-working as a coach and a good coach, particularly defensively, in both football and basketball. Like most coaches, he won with good kids and didn't fare as well with average kids. He had a passion for the game, but I do not think he had a passion for his athletes. However, from '62-'64 he was superb both as a coach and, I think, as a human being. Some of the players from the '64 team informed me they were afraid of him and I think that *added* to their good relationship. He was not personable because he either did not know or did not care about current events or what else was going on in school. In fact, I think he was jealous of other activities. I used to sing at the concerts and programs such as Christmas events and he would tease me sarcastically almost in a mean manner, inquiring, 'Why would I do such things and how was this helping me on the basketball court?'"

Harold Chappell, a 1951 grad and athlete from Wilson's early years, had a much different take on Wilson than Crubaugh. "I was coached in both football and basketball by John 'Weenie' Wilson. During this time frame (1947-51) he taught me a great deal about life, success, the fair treatment of others and tenacity. I wasn't afraid of him, but I knew when he told you something, you better listen. I remember as a just-turned sophomore playing in my first varsity football game and missing a touchdown by only a few inches. He took me aside, (and I thought I might be in for a 'rear-chewing' episode), but instead he told me that with a little extra effort I would have scored. The MESSAGE, always give maximum effort to whatever the task may be. I never forgot that, and it carried over to adulthood that anything less than that is unacceptable. When I first met Weenie Wilson, he looked about 6'7" and a mean guy you better not cross. However, once you got to know him, he was really 5'7" and a wonderful, compassionate, reality-based teacher and coach whom I'll never forget."

Dr. Rolf Lulloff is a 1960 graduate of Dodgeville who played football and basketball under Wilson and competed in track. I asked him to assess Wilson's coaching style. "Weenie (I should call him 'Coach' out of respect) was a task-master as a coach, both in practice and in games. Discipline and perfection were expected at all times. The practices were closed. Nobody was in the gym except for the coaches and players. We all knew we were going to be run hard for usually two hours. He could be and often was profane. Four-letter words were not unusual, yet most of us knew that was his style and not unusual for many coaches of that vintage 'a la Bobby Knight.' He could be harder on some players than others, but we all caught 'hell' from him from time to time, especially if it would help us be better. We would bite our tongues, you never talked back to him. When you graduated you felt he was really trying to make you a better athlete but, more importantly, a better person. At least that is how I felt, and I think most of us share that feeling."

Forward Corky Evans, a former minor-league player, cited in Jim Bouton's baseball classic, *Ball Four*, added this, "If we played well, he told us; and vice-versa! He held nothing back. He wanted us to grow up and be accountable individuals." He went on, "Plus we defended Coach to the public when they would talk to us. The public did not like Coach's style. We defended him and he defended us when he was questioned why so-and-so was playing."

Mike Collins, a 1964 team member put it this way: "Not sure if I liked him, but I did respect him. He seemed to have so much 'power' and influence over us that, to say the least, he was intimidating. He just oozed that he knew best and that BB was the only thing we should concern ourselves with. It wasn't just the win at all cost but if you stick to fundamentals and remain disciplined then good things will come."

"We hated to play for him, but as we became members of the real world we knew that what he had been trying to do was make men out of boys," 1967 grad Denny Rundle says of Wilson. "We all think of him often and the lessons of life often he taught us. He was truly an amazing person for his stature and what he accomplished on and off the field."

Kramer Rock of the 1964 team sums up Coach Wilson and the role the man played in his life: "A demanding taskmaster, he had experienced sports success. He loved personal accolades; he was a big fish in a little pond, which served his ego. He had the same weakness of any man in his 50s then and today. He lived by his own set of values and did his best to convey those values and mores to us. He was honorable, in that he served in the Navy during WWII, when he likely could have found a way not to.

Coach had a Napoleonic streak, in my opinion. He wasn't of physical substance, but coached big. It was his way or the highway, when it came to playing for him. He ran his teams as a self-appointed dictator. That style worked then. We had little else to aspire to or apply our energies.

Sports were our outlet. Literally, sports were the only game in town, if you allow the word play. Did he have a role in my life? You bet. But, some folks deified him. I didn't and still haven't. Wilson, as I remember, was slow to complement, quick to condemn. He was not of the today mindset of building self-esteem through self-indulgent praise and acclamation."

There is a fine line between love and hate. When we love what we are doing but apply our standard to other people, it can cause problems. Some psychologists believe that a love-hate relationship between a coach and players is one of unavoidable acceptance. Such a dynamic, which can remain at an immature level, is more common than we may think. How the relationship is tolerated depends on what is being offered by each party. To make this relationship tolerable, each party must contribute something that the other wants or values. Such relationships are not as one-sided as we might expect, and are often mutually satisfying. In the case of a player, being part of a winning (state champion) team, being afforded the opportunity to play in college, peer notoriety, and fame are certainly possible rewards. For a coach, it could be a resume-builder, public acclaim, or possibly knowing that his *methodology* was spot-on or that the end *justified* the means. In the case of the Dodgeville team, each party did have something of great value for the other.

In the final analysis, perhaps Dodgeville's most visible weakness (the player - coach tension) may well have been their greatest strength. It brought the players together and promoted cohesion. Simply, Weenie was Weenie and that was it. A mature group, the players learned to accept him for who he was because they understood he could never ever alter his style. They understood that his behavior was simply part of his DNA. Together, the players erected a mental fortification that deflected Wilson's harsh behavior. Privately they grieved. Publically they went about their business. On numerous occasions they hoped their coach would not approach the third-rail, but instead find a more temperate way to convey himself. Ultimately, they finally came to realize that the one thing that caused them the greatest *difficulty* in their lives was precisely the same thing that gave them their greatest *satisfaction*. As a result, they persevered and accepted Coach Wilson the way he was— and consequently, they were rewarded by achieving at the highest level possible. Even though Wilson was extremely thorny at times, they trusted that he always had their best interests at heart. As player Bob Rock put it, "There were nights when I went home and cried, but we listened to what he said. He got us to where we wanted to go."

It is only natural to ask: How would Coach Wilson fare today? His passion and commitment were boundless. His work ethic was second to none. An extremely direct mentor, he never took shortcuts. Simply, as he saw it, what didn't outright kill a player would make him more proficient as both athlete and person. No doubt in today's world he would have to soften his approach, control his emotions, perhaps even mollycoddle. But going so against the strong grain of his style, could he succeed? And if he did, would he have the same sense of accomplishment as he did with the Dodgers back in 1963 and 1964?

We can only surmise.

Chapter Twelve

We take most from a story what it urges us to feel. The Dodgeville narrative, the talk of a half-century now, is such a tale. It endures because its values endure; they are every bit as relevant today as half a century ago. History continues on in its seemingly random course, yes, but qualities remain. Our species strives for perfection, wants to succeed, to love and be loved, to do the right thing, yet we are each unique and do not always view the world through equal eyes. The Dodgeville Story exhibits both these enduring values and human differences as they express themselves in a pivotal episode in Wisconsin history. As an author, I thought it best to step out of the way and let those who lived the narrative recall its effect on them and the two generations who have come after. It is the voices of these players, coaches and writers especially, that furnish us with such a vivid portrait of the hard work, physical and psychological demands, and sheer excitement and joy of victory. In our current age of turmoil and uncertainty, there are lessons here for all of us to draw. These same voices tell us not only of a unique story but moreover, the story of America.

The following are commentaries by members of the 1964 Dodgeville team that earned the improbable victory. Following them are the remarks of three outstanding Wisconsin writers. Each shared their views on the Dodgeville story and it's legacy. Here are their thoughts.

Kramer Rock – "The championship year was a year of anticipation and exhilaration. It still is so very memorable to me. Even with today's multiple divisions/classes based on enrollment, it's difficult for young people to experience the joy, pride and giddiness of being part of a state champion team, whether basketball or other endeavor.

In our era it was even more difficult. Over 425 high school basketball teams started in early March 1964 with the same goal—become state champion. Winning and losing distilled that number to two and then the state champion—us.

Dodgeville, with fewer than 400 students, took on and beat an urban school of nearly 1,500 students. All in southwest Wisconsin rallied and embraced our team and journey. Our winning allowed thousands from the area to vicariously be part of that championship season.

Beyond the signs (which stood beyond their relevance and weathered badly over the years) posted at entrances to Dodgeville touting the title, our achievement impacted the lives of those 10 years our chronological junior and those countless years our senior. Over the subsequent decades, when asked in casual conversation where I was born and I mention Dodgeville, an amazing number quickly asked "Were you there when they had that great basketball team?" Without gloating, I proudly say, 'Yep, I played on it.' That's pretty darn cool after so many years.

We were pretty straight-laced young men. At the risk of boasting, I say we often were role models, as to how young men were to live and be positive members of society. The basketball experience gave me personal pride and confidence.

It also made me question unilateral authority. I gained belief in myself. I also learned empathy and sensitivity to others' feelings.

To this day, there are people who say how our achievement inspired them to practice hard, believe, dream and aspire to our level of success. I know in talking to many it was not only in sports but also in their lives. I realized later in my life winning that championship was a huge emotional gift for all in southwest Wisconsin.

Even as the years roll by, the achievement remains a part of Dodgeville and its high school's legacy.

Minimal close family remains in Dodgeville. I am but a name on a trophy or other listing to most who see them. Close family generations may remember—for a while. Add to that my modest role on the team and I surely will not be leaving a sports legacy behind.

But I will leave a more important legacy, in my opinion. That legacy is being father to two daughters who love me and have grown into caring, contributing members of our world. I firmly believe our championship-team experience helped prepare me to be able to earn that legacy.

Trophies, championships and sports achievements are great. I have my share of them. But they tarnish, become scrap and are forgotten. I hope being a loyal, loving, caring father to my children will forever remain and shine brightly. I also hope they and their progeny will remember me as a good, loving man who also happened to experience a sports pinnacle."

Corky Evans - "To me this team championship was an accomplishment of hard work. It showed that the 'little guys' can compete with the 'big guys.' I knew the smaller towns were super happy. I feel very honored to have been a part of both of these years. This championship shows that if a group works hard together for a specific purpose one never knows what can happen. We just worked to get better; we worked together very well; there were no uncontrollable egos on the team. This certainly taught me that teamwork can overcome better talent. I'm very big on teamwork on and off the court. The legacy is not to win all the time, but to always give one's best effort and hope for the best. The effort is always a big factor."

Bob Rock - "What we accomplished was quite remarkable and was probably years in making - in the readiness. It meant a lot to me then—just to be a small part of it. It didn't seem like much pressure on a kid (me) to get the ball to someone else. Being on the team probably offered all of us a bit of high school status at the time, but it's like the whole school was on the team. We (the school, the town) shared the season and the championship. It was bigger than the team.

We were basically some humble guys from a small town working as hard as we could to do our jobs, to contribute to something bigger than what happened in a gym. At that time, it gave us our 15 minutes of fame—and that 15 minutes seemed to come around often that spring in 1964 and has come back to the team on occasion over the years. It seems we gained a bit of local immortality if not popularity—offered

is one of the most memorable things to happen in my life. Thinking that only 12 kids in the entire state of Wisconsin got to go home after the basketball season smiling and being the BEST in the entire state, and that I was one of those kids! Unbelievable!! The combination of school and community, with that team is something I will never forget. The excitement and pride everyone had in that team was just so wonderful. I don't know how it affected future generations, but just a few winters ago they had our team back for a game and recognized us between the varsity game and the JV game. The Dodgeville team was a team that the town thought had a chance to go to state, so the place was pretty full. So many of the older generation we grew up with were no longer alive to see us come back, but the return back was so nice for all of us on that team. I felt as if I were living the story of the 1964 State Champs all over again. It made it hard to ever live up to that. It is still something that happened to me that to this day people remember. I am proud to have been on a team with so many wonderful guys. I feel so fortunate to have been a part of the group and proud to be born and raised in Dodgeville. I was called 'Dickie Dodgeville' while in college, as most of my friends connected me with being from the town that won state and I was on that team. Many of the kids would tell their parents' friends that 'this is my friend Dick... he played on the Dodgeville team in '64!' It never got old, and felt very good. I felt I was a little bit of Weenie Wilson as a coach, and demanded the same types of character qualities I grew up on."

Pat Flynn - "It was the satisfaction that all the work and effort put forth into this endeavor by my teammates and I paid dividends of being recognized as the best basketball team in the state of Wisconsin. It also meant personal recognition and the opportunity to go to college on an athletic scholarship. I think it helped the basketball program, as it created interest in the younger kids and they had goals to shoot for and realized that there are no limits. Never would I have dreamed the impact of our team. My family and I meet people today who still remember the tournament game and team. It brought recognition and a strong sense of pride for the community. In regard to future generations, it was probably both positive and negative. Positive in the sense that it showed that goals could be met with hard work and teamwork. Negative in the sense that it probably put pressure on future teams, as they would always be measured and compared to our team. I'm extremely proud and still amazed that we did what we did. It has given me a great deal of confidence in life, work, and relationships. I have been in management my entire career and I manage by the team concept. I have tried to use the team concept for everything in my life."

Tony Mooren - Ohio native Tony Mooren received his journalism degree from Marquette University in 1969. He lives in Brookfield with his wife Carol and has three children (Mindy, Matt, and Mike) and six grandchildren. An assistant sports editor for *Waukesha Freeman* from 1970 to 2010, he covered the Packers, Brewers, Bucks, and Marquette Golden Eagles, but his main emphasis was high school sports. He earned several Associated Press and United Press International awards for the best sports 'spot news and feature stories.' He was a fifteen-year member of the Baseball Writers Association. In 2010 he was honored with the U.S.T.A Fred Burns award for his life-time contributions to tennis. Tony still writes part-time for the *Freeman*.

"The feat would seem to be almost impossible today – a small school taking on the state's biggest schools and not only beating them but beating them handily for a state championship.

And yet there it was, Wisconsin's own Hoosiers tale, as small-school Dodgeville won it all in 1964.

The team was smarting from a near-record (22-point) 74-52 loss to Manitowoc in the state title game a year before but put the loss behind it and stormed back to take the gold.

After an opening-round 48-43 over Merrill, Dodgeville then blew out Waukesha 60-40 and Milwaukee North 59-45 for the championship and a perfect 26-0 season.

Eight years later, the state would add a second class and now it has five classes – a dilution that is certainly equitable to the majority of the state's schools – small – but simply doesn't have the drama of the single class all-play of yesteryear.

Sure the small schools were at a literal huge disadvantage and were seldom able to claim state championships, but, when they did, the accomplishment seemed to get everyone talking.

"Huge school wins another state title" isn't much of a

story line. It's kind of a ho-hum, here we go again. Open-enrollment currently adds an entirely new dimension as players can, and often do, choose their school.

There were no such choices in 1964.

Merrill, Waukesha and Milwaukee had their players and Dodgeville had its players. The big-city summer leagues and pickup games prepared large-school top athletes well – but not well enough in 1964.

And that's the endearing and enduring recollection of Dodgeville's improbable run. And it was certainly no fluke. Winning state semi-final and championship games by a total 34-point margin stamped the Dodgers as one of the state's best single-season teams ever.

The team's final 26-0 record proved that—only the ninth unbeaten champion in the state's then 49-year history and the 26 victories tying the most for an unbeaten team.

The accomplishment simply had it all."

Cliff Christl - worked as a sportswriter in Wisconsin for more than 36 years with papers in Manitowoc, Green Bay and Milwaukee. A native of Green Bay, he has been inducted into both the Wisconsin Basketball Coaches Association and Wisconsin Football Coaches Association halls of fame for his contributions as a writer. In 2009, he received a Distinguished Alumni Award from the University of Wisconsin-Oshkosh. He was named sportswriter of the year in Wisconsin seven times and won numerous other writing awards. In 1999 and 2001, he was honored by the National Sportscasters & Sportswriters Association for best state championship story. "David and Goliath" can meet in the non-conference portion of the schedule, but never in the state tournament because of different enrollments.

I think the player-coach relationship is changing. The Dodgeville players reminisced that they met at the local pool hall before boarding the bus for road trips. It was there they developed more of a relationship with their coach with small talk before the bus arrived to pick them up. Today, I fear there would be less conversation. The players would be too busy texting their girlfriends, friends and parents or playing a video game on their I-Pad and would be too busy to carry on a conversation with the coach. Also, Coach Wilson used player-coach tension to drive his team to remarkable heights. Although there are exceptions, I do not believe those tactics are as successful today. Coach Wilson would have to probably tone down his methods today, and I have to question if he would have been as successful.

Finally, there was no mention of the Dodgeville kids specializing in one sport, playing AAU basketball in the off-season, or Weenie Wilson having to meet with pressure groups who were concerned with someone's lack of playing time or the coaches' playing style. There was no mention of hurting someone's self-esteem, "Helicopter Parents," or coach Wilson costing someone a college scholarship by the limitations in the Dodgeville offensive scheme. The world of athletics changed since 1964, and some of these changes were positive and some were negative. The reader can decide after reading Rick's book, whether the positives outweighed the negatives."

Epilogue

As we walk the path of life, we do so at our own peril. From our first steps we experiment and assess our abilities and build our self-concepts on the feedback we receive along the way. We soon find we are part of a human framework that judges and steers our every act, envelops virtually all parts of our being. How we react and engage others largely determines our successes, our failures, our destiny.

As we travel this path through and out of adolescence, we encounter others who set great examples, an exemplary few who refuse to live their lives plainly and mundanely and spend their years answering the vital question: How can I make a difference? John "Weenie" Wilson was one of those people. By answering the call, by building a life of distinction in his own right, John Wilson prompted others to become role models for the next generation and to mentor a new cohort of young people, all linked by a common love—that of sport. Who can doubt? The qualities of an accomplished, dedicated coach make an enormous difference for a team, for a community.

To make others believe in their own ultimate success, a coach must have a proven track record and a deep knowledge of the game. He must lead from his heart. He must be an active decision-maker willing to step out of the box to imagine and implement systems that are timely, relevant, and unique.

Who better to train Dodgeville's young champions-to-be than one who had excelled at and coached a variety of sports and who based his philosophy of sport on a rejection of the specialization that stifles so much human potential? Such an open vision encouraged the cross-over effect to govern his athletes and make them all the more well-rounded. Thus, the sum of their athletic skills came to exceed the team's parts.

Wilson set a high standard. He broke down young men, freed them of pretense, then rebuilt them in his likeness, via his superior set of values. A formula for life success took shape—a solid grab-bag of fundamentals and hard, hard work. Like young recruits, the players were compelled to bond military-style amid a belief that no one was more important than any another. These athletes matured quickly because they understood that this same intangible formula would breed their greater success. Like one's never-forgotten first love, this success created a deep and lasting impression: Naïve and vulnerable young men endured a regimen full of demands based on tough love that resulted in player-coach tension. Not in spite of it but because of it they grew mentally and physically strong and came to play like men. Their inner strength, resolve, and will to win captured the hearts of a community and a state. A sense of pride developed that would last forever—Dodgeville pride.

Yes, it is the broader message here that we must acknowledge and cherish. When the heart serves as the basis for a philosophy, the soul can work wonders. Weenie Wilson spent his whole life tirelessly teaching and coaching for his family, the people of Dodgeville. A master coach, Wilson built not only a foundation for sports but a foundation for life, something ceaseless, eternal, that touches us all. A legacy now half a century old is still alive today. In the end, the final judge of each of us is how valued have been our years on earth to help others, our kind words and deeds and instructions to the young, the values we stand for, how we carry the standard set by others farther down the playing field. Our deeds based on our dreams allow others, in turn, to pursue their own.

Come March, I always think of Dodgeville. I think of that time so close to my own young heart. The city itself has come to be synonymous with Wisconsin high school basketball. Yes, fifty years have now passed, yet the memory remains vivid and the values passed on unequalled. What I learned from it then I still discover from it today, and more. Basketball is much, much more than a game. It's a living, breathing metaphor for hard work, sportsmanship, courage, pride—human success. It's about a coach who fought for his dream with every scrap of intensity, ignoring parochial criticisms. It's about a team that manifested its destiny against overwhelming odds, in a one-size-fits-all competition. It's about a magical group of athletes who, somehow convened at precisely the right time and under the tutelage of this coach, were transformed into men almost overnight. For this they were rewarded with the biggest prize in high school basketball.

One might ask: Was it fate? Many would say that on

March 21, 1964, fate itself replied with a resounding "Yes!"

An athlete or coach on the big stage never really knows who is watching him. Moreover, one's first impression and his deeds can influence others quite immensely. That day in our home in 1963, watching and deciding that Dodgeville would be "my team," I wasn't deciding that the Dodgers would be my team for that day or that tournament but for my longer life and purpose. I would strive to live my life as best I could according to the principles the players demonstrated—giving, love for one another, a never-give-up attitude, and all that hard, hard work. As a young boy myself, I began to realize that, if you can dream it, you can make it happen. Could all this ever happen again? Most likely not. Times are much different now. Let's appreciate the fact that it did happen in 1964. I can attest that I saw it with my own eyes and my heart, too, was captured.

Where Are They Now?

John "Weenie" Wilson - After the championship victory of 1964, John "Weenie" Wilson continued to teach and coach at Dodgeville for the next four years. On October 30, 1968 he suffered a heart attack just prior to a physical education class at Dodgeville and passed away shortly after. Wilson, who spent 23 years at Dodgeville, was an accomplished athlete and a dedicated, hardworking teacher who instilled a lifelong love of sport in his students and athletes. Through the years his teams won numerous championships and awards, his biggest being the 1964 state basketball championship when his Dodger team defeated Milwaukee North by a score of 59-45. Coach Wilson is the only coach to be enshrined in the Wisconsin Coaches Association Hall of Fame in football, basketball and baseball. He was inducted into the Dodgeville Hall of Fame in 2010 and has left a legacy of pride at Dodgeville. Serving in World War II, he spent five years in the Navy prior to taking the only teaching and coaching position he would ever hold. He was survived by his wife of 27 years, Blanche, who passed away on May 1, 1994, at age 77.

James (Joe) Whitford - Joe graduated from UW-Platteville in 1959 and later earned a Master's degree in safety education from UW-Whitewater. After teaching industrial arts and coaching at Dodgeville from 1959-1964, the Whitford family moved to Waterford. Here Joe taught industrial arts and driver's education from 1964 to 1986. At Waterford Joe was involved in athletics immediately. He coached basketball, football, and volleyball and was the head baseball and softball coach. In 1977 Joe became the head girls' basketball coach. He guided his team to a state championship in 1985, compiling a nine-year record of 155-45. His last team, ranked number one all year long, won 25 consecutive games before losing the state title. Joe was a member of St. Peter's Lutheran Church. A veteran, he served in the army during the Korean Conflict and was a 33-year member of the Army Reserve 84th Division. Joe was a commander of the Essman-Schroeder American Legion Post in Waterford. Whitford Park in Waterford is named in his honor. Joe passed away from cancer on February 2, 1986, at St. Luke's Hospital in Racine, surrounded by his loving family.

Bob Anderson - After receiving his Bachelor's degree from the University of Wisconsin, Bob enlisted in the U.S. Navy. A career Navy Officer for thirty-two years, he is now working with the Navy as a civilian. Bob is employed as the director of an office that works with Hollywood in the entertainment industry.

Curt Anderson - After graduating from DHS Curt went to MATC in Madison. At the present time he is still a self-employed carpenter and continues to live in Dodgeville.

Curt is married to Sharon and they have two daughters— Kate & Molly. Both daughters attended UW-Eau Claire and work in the Twin Cities area in early childhood-special education and social work.

Curt enjoys photography and gardening and does some volunteer work.

Rick Brown - After graduation Rick accepted a full athletic scholarship to Arizona State University. After one year, he returned to Wisconsin and attended Ripon College, where he earned his degree in Theater Arts. He has worked in the film industry and as an iron-worker most of his life. He continues to work, as he finds it difficult to retire. Rick loves the outdoors and has a place in Lake of the Woods, Canada, where the walleyes are plentiful. He remembers his days in Dodgeville fondly. He feels very fortunate to have been raised in the community.

Tom Brunker - Tom is retired now. He and his wife, Annie, live in Barneveld. They have stayed in southern Wisconsin all their lives. They are close to nearly all of their family, including twelve grandkids, all within an hour of them. The oldest is 16 and the youngest is 18 months.

Something ironic: Tom was probably the shortest guy (5'6") on the basketball team at D.H.S. He has a seventh-grade grandson who is 6'1". His grandson has already played A.A.U. basketball in four states. Tom never played basketball until he was in eighth grade.

Tom was forced to retire ten years ago in 2003. He contracted a rare brain illness called neurosarcoidosis. It took 24 doctors, 4 M.R.I.'s, 6 spinal taps and several other tests to diagnose it. Tom beat it after brain surgery and several months of medication! He now works part-time at his stepson's pizza place in Mt. Horeb.

Bobby Campbell - Robert G. (Bobby) Campbell, Jr., age thirty-one, passed away in his sleep on Wednesday, September 21, 1977. Born June 12, 1946, the son of Robert Campbell, Sr., and the former Rhoda Blied, Bobby was a life-long Dodgeville resident and a 1964 Dodgeville High grad. He earned a BA in business administration from Milton College and went into partnership with his dad at Campbell's Dry Goods Store. A member of the Plymouth Congregational United Church of Christ and a church trustee, Bobby also joined the Dodgeville Chamber of Commerce and served as president of the 1976 DUFI (Dodgeville United Fund Incorporated.) He was survived by his parents and grandparents, Mr. and Mrs. Walter Blied of Dodgeville, formerly of Madison, and preceded in death by his other grandparents, Mr. and Mrs. Albert R. Campbell. Funeral services were at the Plymouth Congregational United Church of Christ, with the Reverend David Roberts officiating. Burial was at Dodgeville's Eastside Cemetery.

Close friend Mike Reilly writes of an amazing excursion a year before Bobby's passing. "Bobby, Curt Anderson, I, and a newbie in town, Norm Draeger, went on a Scandinavian Cruise to England, Scotland, Norway, Sweden, and Denmark for three weeks in 1976," Reilly reports. "We had a great time seeing castles and other historic sites and visiting a share of local pubs and taverns. We even watched the King of Sweden's funeral procession and saw the new King, who was younger than even we were."

Bobby is missed and will forever be in the hearts of his Dodgeville team.

Mike Collins - Mike has been blissfully married to his second wife Carla for 17 years and they reside in McFarland, WI. He has a son and daughter, and Carla has twin daughters and a son, who have blessed them with 9 grandchildren. Mike retired in 2011 after 40 years at the University of Wisconsin Hospital and Clinics as a Clinical Assistant Professor of Pharmacy and Neurology and specialized in the treatment of epilepsy. He is an avid fisherman and on the pro staff for a number of companies for salmon fishing. He and Carla met dancing and are founding members of the Madison West Coast Swing Club.

Corky Evans - Corky graduated from Dodgeville High School in 1964 and attended UW-Madison for one year (1964-65) on a baseball scholarship. In January, 1966, he signed a professional baseball contract with the Baltimore Orioles. Corky played six years in the minors with three different organizations before giving it up. He then went back to school at age 25 and graduated from Winona State (MN) at age 28. In 1980, he received a Masters degree. At age 28, Corky started teaching sixth grade in New London, Wi., where he taught for 27 years. He took early retirement at age 55.

Corky is happily married to Eileen for 43 years. They have a son, Cory, and a daughter, Tatum, and two super grandchildren, Sybil and Gordon (Catherine: daughter-in-law, Todd: son-in-law). Presently he is relaxing and enjoys following sports in retirement life.

Patrick Flynn - Patrick lives in LaGrange, Georgia, and is married to a wonderful woman (Lynn), has two wonderful children (Brian & Kristin), six grandchildren, and two great-grandchildren. He graduated from Milton College in Milton, Wisconsin, with a degree in Business Administration and has worked in Healthcare Management for 44 years in Wisconsin, Florida, Illinois, New York, and Georgia. Patrick is currently employed by Emory Clark-Holder Clinic as Chief Financial Officer and plays golf as a weekend activity.

Bruce Harrison - Bruce has loved and supported his wonderful family, pursued and earned a successful career in the field of golf, traveled, met many good people and enjoyed long friendships, and tried to do his best in every circumstance. He and his wife Christine have three children: Anthony (Esther) who has three children (Preston, Dorothy, Benjamin), Todd (Julie) who has two children (Jacob, Ellie), and Jacqueline, who is mentally handicapped and lives with Mom and Dad in Port St. Lucie, Florida where they have resided for the last 36+ years.

Bob Rock - In 1968 Rock was named to "Who's Who in American Colleges and Universities" during the year he was captain of the St. Norbert basketball team, playing there on scholarship. Following a successful college sports and academic career, Rock served in the US Army in Vietnam. In June, 1970, he returned, highly decorated, from his duty with the 101st Airborne Division to complete an additional 10 years in the US Army Reserve.

He is the father of three and grandfather of six. In his semi-retirement, he stays busy with his consulting business, making memories as a grandfather along with his hobbies of hiking, writing and photography.

For over twenty years Rock has represented several incentive marketing companies, while serving dozens of corporations, delivering expertise in the areas of domestic and world-wide travel destinations, designing and implementing incentive programs, motivating thousands of participants to attain increased sales as well as non-sales achievements.

Kramer Rock - After earning a Bachelor's degree from the University of Wisconsin-Madison and active military duty, he joined Carnation Company as division advertising manager. He then worked in sales and management in the industrial/agricultural equipment sectors prior to becoming a business owner.

He is president/owner of Temployment, Inc., in Green Bay, Wi. Temployment, Inc., a staffing services firm, has provided personnel for the short-term and planned staffing needs of Green Bay area business, industry, education and government since 1979.

He has led, as board chair, many not-for-profits in Green Bay. They range from the inaugural Women's Professional Golf Tour (now the Legends Tour) tourneys in Green Bay, to founding board chair of a performing arts venue. He served as a member of the Greater Green Bay Community Foundation board, as well as the senior advisory board of Junior Achievement. He is board chair of the Neville Public

Museum Foundation. He is a board member of the Green Bay Packers Hall of Fame, as well as a member of the UW-Green Bay Council of Trustees and other not-for-profits.

Married to Carolyn, he has two daughters, Emily K., born in 1987, and Maggie Mae, born in 1990. He has a special interest in history, the arts and helping the aging. He actively participates in the political process and was a candidate for the Wisconsin senate. A licensed pilot, he enjoys recreational flying. He also enjoys reading, golfing and following sports.

He believes his greatest achievement in life is being father to two daughters who love him and have grown into caring, contributing members of our world.

Tom Schleck - Tom graduated from the UW-Madison in Finance in 1970 and joined the Bank of America in California. He met his wife at the Bank of America and married in 1973. They raised four children who now live in California, Texas and Hawaii. So far they have produced five grandchildren! After 11 years as a corporate banker, Tom joined one of his customers in the healthcare industry as its treasurer. The remainder of his career was spent in the healthcare industry as a financial officer. He is now retired and lives with his wife in Montecito, Ca., a small community in the Santa Barbara area.

Dick Stephens - Dick attended University of Wisconsin-Whitewater from 1965 until graduation in January 1970. He then taught a half year at Zion-Benton High School in Zion, Il. in spring of 1970. He next taught at Schaumburg High School in Schaumburg, Il. from August of 1970 until June

2002. Dick was a 4-year starting pitcher on the Whitewater baseball team, and he played 2 years of basketball for Whitewater as well. Dick was head baseball coach at Schaumburg High for 15 years, coached boys basketball for 7 years, girls basketball for 22, and boys golf for 27 years.

He is married with 2 daughters and currently lives in St. Charles, Il. Having daughters brought Dick to fast-pitch softball with the Wasco Diamond travel softball program, where he coached for 12 years. He is a long-time Badger, Packer, and Brewer fan, and goes to many of their games, along with high school basketball and softball games. Sports is a big part of his life, along with his family, and he is so very proud to be from Dodgeville, Wi.

Larry Wagner - Larry attended Iowa State University in Ames, Ia, where he graduated with an Engineering and Architecture degree. In 1968, he married Mary Jo Collins of Dodgeville. Larry worked with Marshall Erdman in Madison, from 1968 to 1974. In 1974 he moved back to Dodgeville to help his father-in-law run Collins & Hying Plumbing & Heating. Here Larry worked for 36 years and was the owner for the last 30 years. On August 15, 1992, Larry married Marcia May. Larry has four children. Always having a passion for golf, he was a member of the Dodge-Point Country Club. Larry earned many awards in golf and was inducted into the Dodge-Point Country Club Hall of Fame in July of 2010. Larry passed away on September 23, 2010, at his home while surrounded by his loving family.

References

A special thanks to the following publications for allowing me to venture back into their achieves and utilize their historical commentary and analysis which has added immeasurably to this story.

Dodger Highlife: Mar, 1964

Dodgeville Chronicle: Nov, 1963–Sep, 2010

Dubuque Telegraph Herald: Mar, 1964

Green Bay Press-Gazette: Apr, 2013

La Crosse Tribune: Mar, 1964

Madison Capital Times: Mar, 1963; Mar, 1964

Milwaukee Journal–Sentinel: Mar, 1963; Mar, 1964

Mishler, Todd. Great Moments in Wisconsin Sports. Black Earth, WI.: Trails Books, 2004

Prep Illustrated: Dec, 1963, Apr, 1964

Rhinelander Daily News: Mar, 1964

Wisconsin Basketball News: Mar, 2004

Wisconsin State Journal: Sep, 1935; Mar, 1964; Apr, 1964

Appendix

1933 Richland Center High School Football Team

John Wilson - Top Row, 3rd from right

Courtesy of Farness Studios & Richland Center High School

John Wilson
Basketball player at Richland Center High School 1933

Courtesy of the Wilson Family

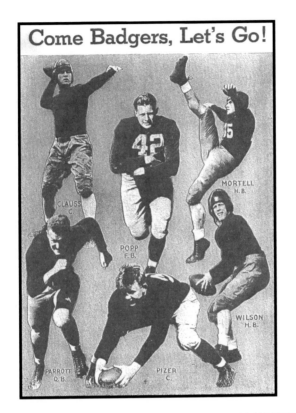

Wisconsin Official Football Program 10/19/1935

John Wilson - bottom right

Courtesy of the University of Wisconsin

Dodgeville High School 1962-63

Courtesy of Berard Photography and the Dodgeville Chronicle

Dodgeville Basketball Team 1962-63

Front Row: Manager Bob Campbell, Tom Brunker, Dennis Morgan, Tom Hughes, Bruce Harrison, Scott Wichman, Steve Rasmussen, Ron Dickinson, Ron Maines, Bob Rock.
Back Row: Coach John Wilson, Duane Honerbaum, Corky Evans, David Johanning, Brian Olson, Curtis Anderson, Pat Flynn, Pat Reilly, Bill Polkinghorn, Rick Brown, John Crubaugh (Asst. Coach).

Courtesy of Berard Photography and the Dodgeville Chronicle

State Runner-up Trophy 1963

Courtesy of the WIAA & Dodgeville High School

Dodgeville Track Team 1963

Kneeling: Coach Dave Spies, Manager Bob Campbell, Coach Joe Whitford. **Front Row:** Paul Richards, Doug Roh, Jim Rohowetz, Jim Keyes, Gary Butteris, Greg Weier, Lyle Richardson, Rick Jeske, Tom Chappell, Vern Abdoo, William Toay, Mike Ruppert, Tim Cretney. **Second Row:** William Jones, Tom Hughes, David Fitzsimons, Dennis Thomas, Terry Rule, Paul Butteris, William Hanson, Roger Black, Gary Gullickson, Dennis Wilkinson, Ron Maines, Tom Rowe, Fred Schroeder. **Third Row:** David Price, Steve Rasmussen, Jim Maxon, Tom Metcalf, Tom Schleck, Bob Boldt, Bob Rundle, Dan Stombaugh, Bill Polkinghorn, Rick Brown, Pat Flynn, Steve Wolenec.

Courtesy of Berard Photography and the Dodgeville Chronicle

Dodgeville Baseball Team 1963

Front Row: Tom Martin, Bill Reese, Gene Smith, Joe Meudt, Lavon Roberts, Dennis Esch, Dan Halverson, Ed Hirsch, Greg Davis, Randy Jackson. **Second Row:** DuWayne Wenger, Bruce Rundle, Joe Evans, Mike Gust, Jerry Weier, Bob Zweifel, Bruce Harrison, Mark James, Dennis Morgan, Larry Wagner.
Third Row: Coach Wilson, Jeff Schroeder, Ron Boettcher, Jon Jacka, Bob Fitzsimons, Scott Wichmann, Bill Rock, Doug Loy, Gary Johnson, Dick Stephens, Ken Johanning, Steve Schroeder, Al Jacobson. **Fourth Row:** Pat Reilly, Kramer Rock, Brian Olson, Duane Honerbaum, Corky Evans, David Johanning, Gary Rundle, Bob Rock, Tom Watkins, Gary Storzbach.

Courtesy of Berard Photography and the Dodgeville Chronicle

Dodgeville Golf Team 1963

Steve Larson, Nat Cerutti, Mike Reilly, Mr. Bomhoff, Mike
Collins, Rodger Perkins, Bob Anderson, John Nelson

Courtesy of Berard Photography and the Dodgeville Chronicle

New Dodgeville High School 1963-64

Courtesy of Berard Photography and the Dodgeville Chronicle

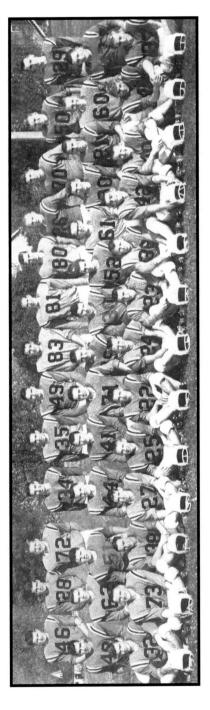

Dodgeville Football Team 1963

Front Row: Ken Johanning, Bill Rock, Jim Rohowetz, Bill Harris, Tom Chappell, Bill Hanson, Bruce Harrison, Bill Reese, Steve Schroeder, Gary Tyrer, Mike Ruppert, Tim Cretney, Lavon Roberts. **Second Row:** DuWayne Wenger, Dennis Esch, Dennis Thomas, Larry Wagner, Terry Johnson, David Fitzsimons, Dennis Wilkinson, Gene Smith, Gary Butteris, Mike Collins, Bob Wilson, Dick Stephens, Curt Prideaux, Bob McGraw. **Third Row:** Douglas Loy, Steve Rasmussen, John Jacka, Bob Rock, Tom Schleck, Jim Maxon, Danny Stombaugh, Rick Brown, Pat Flynn, Corky Evans, Bob Rundle, Bob Fitzsimons, Bob Boldt.

Courtesy of Berard Photography and the Dodgeville Chronicle

Dodgeville Wrestling Team 1963-64

Kneeling: Martin Alvstad, Mike Ryan. **Front Row:** Jim Rowe, Gary Tyrer, Gary Ellenbolt, Paul Rochon, Dwight Cutler, John Jones, Jim Rohowetz, Jeff Schroeder, Rick Rasmussen, Arthur Humbert, Tom Martin, John McDermott. **Second Row:** Dick McCluskey, Dennis Schaack, Gene Smith, Dennis Thomas, Larry Roberts, Dallas Stenner, Tim Cretney, Jim Lucas, Dennis Phillips, Terry Rule, Greg Weier, Ed Hirsch, Gary Garthwait, Greg Davis. **Third Row:** Coach Heim, Dennis Landen, Ron Squire, Bob Rundle, Ron Boettcher, Steve Rasmussen, Jon Jacka, Curt Prideaux, Bill Hanson, Tom Dettman, Russell Newberry, Harold March, Bob Wilson, Philip Woerpel, Dave Fitzsimons

Courtesy of Berard Photography and the Dodgeville Chronicle

Dodgeville Basketball Team 1963-64

Front Row: Tom Brunker, Mike Collins, Bob Rock, Curt Anderson, Rick Brown, Pat Flynn, Corky Evans, Bruce Harrison, Coach John Wilson. **Back Row:** Manager Bob Anderson, Bill Harris, Craig Brue, Mike Gust, Kramer Rock, Danny Stombaugh, Tom Schleck, Larry Wagner, Ken Johanning, Dick Stephens, Manager Bob Campbell. Not Shown: Steve Schroeder.

Courtesy of Berard Photography and the Dodgeville Chronicle

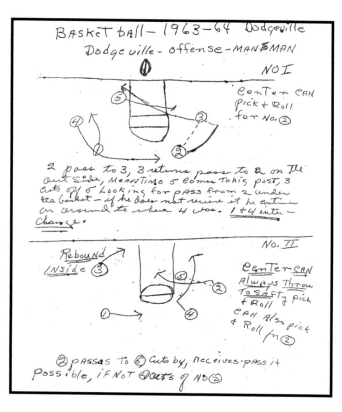

Basket ball – 1963-64 Dodgeville

Dodgeville - offense - MAN TO MAN

NO I

Center can
Pick + Roll
for No. ②

2 pass to 3, 3 returns pass to 2 on the outside, meantime 5 comes to his post, 3 cuts off 5 looking for pass from 2 under the basket – if he does not receive it he continues on around to where 4 was. 1 & 4 interchange.

NO. II

Rebound
Inside ③

Center can
Always throw
to safty pick
+ Roll
Can. Also pick
& Roll for ②

② passes to ⑤ cuts by, receives pass if possible, if not ② cuts off No ②

Wilson's man-to-man offense - 1963-64

Courtesy of Coach Bob Buck

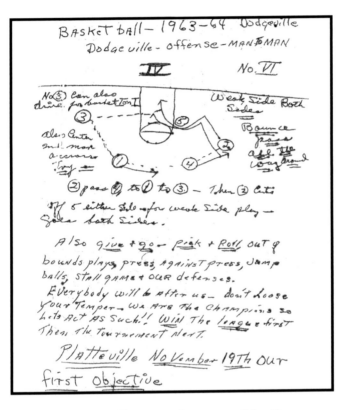

Basketball — 1963-64 Dodgeville

Dodgeville - offense - MAN TO MAN

IV   No. VI

No③ can also
drive for basket on I

③

Weak Side Both
Sides

⑤

Bounce
pass

also Center
2nd man
a-cross

①   ④   ②

all the
way around

② pass ⑤ to ① to ③ — Then ② cuts
off 5 either side — for weak side play —
Goes both sides.

Also give + go — pick + Roll out of
bounds plays, press against press, Jump
balls, stall game + our defenses.

Everybody will be after us — don't loose
your Temper — We are the Champions so
lets act as such!! Win The league first
Then The Tournament Next.

Platteville November 19th our
first objective

**Additional offense and season objectives -
Platteville, league, then tournament 1963-64**

Courtesy of Coach Bob Buck

Dodgeville's Faithful Cheerleaders 1963-1964

Ginnie Arthur	Donna Schill	Anne Ayers
Marjorie Mathison	Mary Keyes	Betty Baumgardt

Courtesy of Berard Photography and the Dodgeville Chronicle

Tourney Squad poses with Dodgeville fire truck
3/18/1964

Courtesy of Berard Photography and the Dodgeville Chronicle

Neighboring communities showing Dodger support
3/18/1964

Courtesy of Berard Photography and the Dodgeville Chronicle

At State - Merrill versus Dodgeville 3/19/1964

Courtesy of Berard Photography and the Dodgeville Chronicle

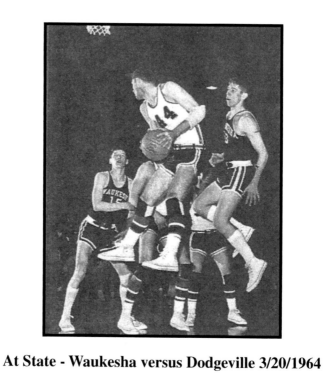

At State - Waukesha versus Dodgeville 3/20/1964

Courtesy of Berard Photography and the Dodgeville Chronicle

**Dodgeville Cheerleaders arriving at Championship
Game 3/21/1964**

Courtesy of Berard Photography and the Dodgeville Chronicle

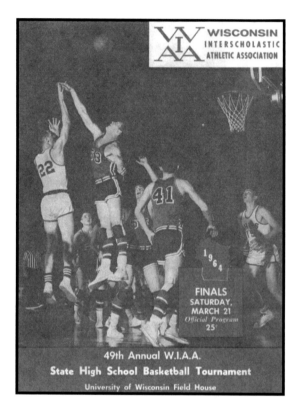

State Finals Program 3/21/64

Courtesy of the WIAA

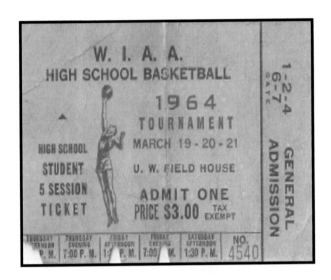

North - Dodgeville Ticket Stub 3/21/1964

Courtesy of Jan (Kobbervig) Uselmann

At State - Milwaukee North versus Dodgeville
3/21/1964

Courtesy of Berard Photography and the Dodgeville Chronicle

Dodgeville cheerleaders and crowd urging their team on

Courtesy of Berard Photography and the Dodgeville Chronicle

**Accepting the State Championship Trophy in Madison
3/21/1964**

Courtesy of Berard Photography and the Dodgeville Chronicle

State Championship Trophy 3/21/1964

Courtesy of the WIAA & Dodgeville High School

Only five Dodgeville players took the floor in the 1964 Championship Game

Bob Rock, Bruce Harrison, Corky Evans,
Pat Flynn, Rick Brown

Courtesy of Berard Photography and the Dodgeville Chronicle

**Wilson addressing the Dodgeville crowd of well-wishers
in Dodgeville 3/21/1964**

Courtesy of Berard Photography and the Dodgeville Chronicle

Coach Wilson and team take to the stage 3/21/1964

Courtesy of Berard Photography and the Dodgeville Chronicle

Dodgeville parents honored 3/21/1964

Courtesy of Berard Photography and the Dodgeville Chronicle

Dodgeville celebration 3/21/1964

Courtesy of Berard Photography and the Dodgeville Chronicle

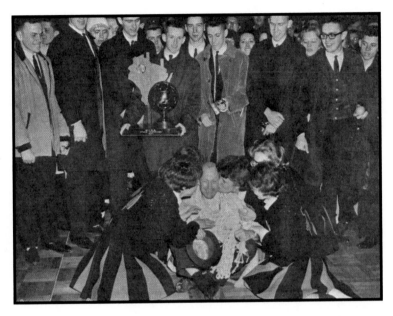

Cheerleaders showing appreciation for Coach Wilson

Courtesy of Berard Photography and the Dodgeville Chronicle

Jt. Res. No. 95, S.

No.————————, 1963

A JOINT RESOLUTION

Congratulating the Dodgeville High School basketball team on winning the 1964 state high school basketball championship.

————————

WHEREAS, the Dodgeville High School basketball team won the 1964 state high school basketball championship at the University of Wisconsin Field House on March 21, 1964, by beating Milwaukee North High School by a score of 59 to 45; and

WHEREAS, the Dodgeville team compiled a record of 26 consecutive wins and became only the ninth champion to go through a season undefeated; and

WHEREAS, Coach John (Weenie) Wilson's wonders were one of the finest defensive clubs seen in years, particularly in state tournament play where they held all 9 opponents to less than 50 points and, in the championship game, held Milwaukee North to one-half its usual scoring average; and

WHEREAS, this team and its fine coach, in winning the tournament this year and in finishing second last year, captured the hearts of all Wisconsinites and proved that a little school can still produce mighty champions; now, therefore, be it

Resolved by the senate, the assembly concurring, That the legislature applauds Coach John Wilson and the members of the Dodgeville High School basketball team—Pat Flynn, Rick Brown, Bruce Harrison, Carlos Evans, Bob Rock, Curt Anderson, Tom Brunker, Dick Stephens, Tom Schleck, Ken Johanning, Kramer Rock and Mike Gust—on winning the 1964 state high school basketball championship; and, be it further

Resolved, That properly attested copies of this resolution be transmitted to Coach Wilson and to each member of the Dodgeville team.

PRESIDENT OF THE SENATE.   SPEAKER OF THE ASSEMBLY.

CHIEF CLERK OF THE SENATE.   CHIEF CLERK OF THE ASSEMBLY.

State of Wisconsin - Joint Resolution 3/21/1964

Courtesy of Dodgeville High School

Dodgeville Track Team 1964

Front Row: Eric Rasmussen, Terri Venden, Jerry Trulen, Jim Rohowetz, Paul Rochen, Arthur Humbert, Dwight Cutler, John McDermott, Martin Alvstad, Glen Rossing, Henry Edl, Mike Ryan. **Second Row:** Rick Jeske, Greg Weier, Tom Anderson, Jim Keyes, Ed Hirsch, Dennis Rundle, Doug Roh, Jim Rowe, Perry Schaak, David Foley, Will Rule, Jeff Schroeder, Mr. Whitford. **Third Row:** Bill Hanson, Bob Wilson, Dennis Schaack, Paul Butteris, Phillip Woerpel, Darrell March, Jerome Brokish, Mike Matarresse, Terry Rule, Mark Masters, Dennis Thomas, Tom Chappell. **Back Row:** Bob Boldt, Tom Schleck, Steve Rasmussen, Curt Anderson, Jim Maxon, Rick Brown, Dan Stombaugh, Tom Metcalf, Bob Rundle, Dennis Wilkinson, Tom Rowe, Tom Dettman, Larry Roberts.

Courtesy of Berard Photography and the Dodgeville Chronicle

Dodgeville Golf Team 1964

Kneeling: Mike Collins, John Nelson, Roger Perkins, Steve Larson, Craig Brue, Mike Reilly. **Standing:** Fred Stratman, Bob Anderson, Nat Cerutti, Mr. Cook, Bob Dunbar, Steve Erickson, Paul Wiese.

Courtesy of Berard Photography and the Dodgeville Chronicle

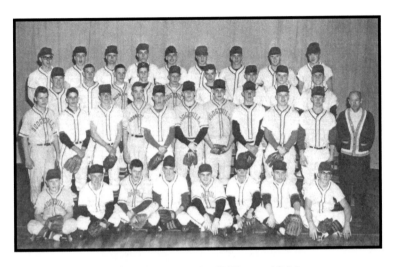

Dodgeville Baseball Team 1964

Front Row: Teddy Evans, Tom Martin, Mike Starczynski, Bill Harris, Greg Davis, Jack Stephens, Tom Brunker, Dennis Esch. **Second Row:** Jim Butteris, Randy Jackson, Doug Murphy, Dan Halverson, Jeff Heibel, Craig Heibel, Mark Van Epps, Marc Higgins, Joe Evans, Bruce Harrison, Coach John Wilson. **Third Row:** Gene Smith, Gary Johnson, Tom Watkins, Dick Stephens, Steve Schroeder, Ken Johanning, Mike Gust, Bill Rock, Larry Wagner. **Back Row:** Curt Prideaux, Jon Jacka, Ron Boettcher, Bruce Rundle, Bob Fitzsimons, Doug Loy, Bob Rock, Corky Evans, Kramer Rock.

Courtesy of Berard Photography and the Dodgeville Chronicle

Kramer Rock and the Darlington Beauty - April, 1964

Courtesy of the Dodgeville Junior Prom Couple

5 Starters - 10 Year Reunion, 1974

Bob Rock, Bruce Harrison, Corky Evans,
Pat Flynn, Rick Brown

Courtesy of Berard Photography and the Dodgeville Chronicle

Team 46 Year Reunion - 2010

Sitting: Dick Stephens, Tom Brunker, Bruce Harrison, Bob Rock. **Standing:** Curt Anderson, Ken Johanning, Mike Collins, Corky Evans, Rick Brown, Pat Flynn, Kramer Rock

Courtesy of Berard Photography and the Dodgeville Chronicle